The Art of Quantum Trading ∞ John Carballar

Copyright © 2024 John Carballar

All rights reserved

No part of this book may be reproduced, stored or transmitted in any form or by any means, electronic, mechanical, photocopying, recording or otherwise, without the prior written permission of the author, except in the case of brief quotations used in reviews or critical articles.

This book is a work of nonfiction. Names, characters, places and incidents are the product of the author's research. Any resemblance to actual persons, living or dead, events or locales is purely coincidental.

First Edition: November/2024

Cover Design by: John Carballar

Printed in the United States of America

INTRODUCTION

Imagine waking up in a dark cell, next to a stranger, with no idea why you're there. When you open your eyes, you realize you're trapped in a vertical prison, *The Hole*, a structure with hundreds of levels stacked on top of each other. On each level, two people, and a platform with food that descends from the top to the bottom, leaving those at the top with the privilege of satiating themselves, while those at the bottom barely receive crumbs if there is anything left. Desperation takes hold of everyone. Those at the top enjoy abundance, those at the bottom suffer scarcity. And amidst all this chaos, violence and hunger, those at the bottom are forced to fight against the most basic human instinct: to survive.

Now, imagine that this hole is not just a prison, but a metaphor for the financial market, where we traders are immersed. Every day, we fight in a system that seems designed so that only a few win while the majority fights for what is left. Those "at the top" – the big institutions, the investment funds, the traders with access to the best information – take their big slices, leaving the rest of us, the retailers, at the mercy of what is left. And when the market goes wild, many falls, exhausted by effort and despair, wondering if they will ever manage to get out of this vicious circle.

But there is a crucial part in *The Hole,* this 2019 Spanish film, that changes the whole story. Goreng, the protagonist, descends deeper and deeper, until he reaches the lowest levels. There, in the depths of the abyss, on the edge of what seems to be total hopelessness, he discovers something unexpected: a message. In the film, that message takes the form of a little girl, a sign that there is something pure and valuable in the midst of chaos, proof that hope exists, even in the darkest of circumstances.

That descent to rock bottom can be interpreted as a journey to the depths of consciousness, the point where we hit rock bottom, both in the market and in our emotional life. As traders, we have been there. We know what it is like to lose everything, to feel like we have descended to the lowest level, both in terms of financial and emotional losses. It is there, at that point, that much give up. But it is precisely in that place that the most important message is found.

That message is that the way up is not just a matter of technique or strategy, but of awareness. It is deep within ourselves that we discover that the keys to surviving and thriving in the market are not just in charts or external tools, such as technical indicators, but in inner strength, in the ability to master our emotions, in the peace of mind so as not to be carried away by panic or greed.

When I hit rock bottom, I understood that the market is a reflection of our mind. When we are trapped in fear, in the need to control the uncontrollable, we become prisoners, like those who inhabit the lowest levels of the pit. But by finding that "message" within ourselves—clarity, emotional control, the awareness that we are bigger than our circumstances—we begin to transform our relationship with the market. We stop fighting it and start flowing with it.

This book is precisely that message. It is not just a guide to navigate the market, but a manual to understand that, although it may seem like we are trapped in an unfair system, we have the power to free ourselves from within. Because, just like in *The Hole*, the real battle is not outside, it is in our minds and in how we face our deepest fears and desires.

My goal is to show you that, although the market may seem like a prison designed to make us fall, it is also the perfect terrain to discover what we are really capable of achieving when we find that message deep within ourselves. Overall, it is not just about surviving in the market, it is about learning to live in peace with it, and with yourself.

Preface

This book is dedicated especially to those who are already trading in the markets, or to those beginners who are looking for answers. But if you have not yet chosen to start trading, I suggest you think carefully before entering, and only do so if you are willing to take it professionally. This business is one of the most difficult in the world, and there is no middle ground: either you go completely bankrupt, or you permanently change your financial situation.

You must be aware of the monumental challenge you are going to face if you decide to enter into trading. It doesn't matter if you are a beginner, have intermediate experience, or are an expert: there is one thing I can assure you right now: you'll lose money. And if it is about losing money, there are many other more fun ways to do it.

Trading is almost like a disease that has no cure; once you're in it, it's challenging to get it out of your head. And, like an incurable disease, the least we can do is learn to live with it. That said, I want to make it clear that this is not a magic book that will guarantee you success or make you a millionaire overnight. But it will teach you how to live with trading, how to integrate it into your daily life, and how to turn it into a tool for growth both in the market and personally.

If you decide to go ahead, welcome to the ride.

The Art of Quantum Trading ∞ John Carballar

INDEX

INTRODUCTION... 2

Chapter I... 8

    Field of Options and Quantum Physics applied to Trading............... 8

    Quantum Superposition and Trading.. 12

    Excessive potential and its influence.. 16

    Strategies to Avoid Excessive Potential... 19

    The Observer and the Collapse of Reality.. 20

    Mind control and the collapse of favorable variants......................... 23

Chapter II... 26

    Pendulums in Trading.. 26

    How destructive pendulums influence trading................................. 33

    How Great Traders Deal With Market Pendulums........................... 36

    How to free yourself from destructive pendulums............................ 38

    Going with the Market: Sinking the Pendulum................................. 44

    Easy solutions to difficult problems... 47

    The Suspended State.. 50

Chapter III.. 54

    The wave of fortune.. 54

    Antipode to the pendulum: There are no constructive pendulums.......... 56

The Boomerang: What you think comes back to you in trading............58

Preparation rituals: Aligning yourself with the Wave of Success in Trading............64

Chapter IV............68

Keep the balance............68

Discontent and self-criticism............72

Emotional Dependencies in Trading............77

Illusions and overconfidence............81

Judgments and Arrogance............86

Comparisons and mentality............90

Feeling of guilt............97

The relationship with money............101

Real goals vs. imposed goals............103

The Trap of Perfection in Trading............106

Inner weight............110

Outer weight............111

    Inner weight in Trading............112

    Outer weight in Trading............112

    Strategies to manage importance............114

From struggle to balance............116

Chapter V............121

Reactive shift..121

Loop of Influence...125

Chapter VI..129

Stream of variants...129

Connecting with the field of variants..132

Pleader, Bitter, and Fighter..136

An alternative to the Fighter..140

How to read the signs?..144

Let it go...148

Chapter I

Field of Options and Quantum Physics applied to Trading

In this first chapter, we will explore the concept of "field of options" and how it connects to theories of quantum physics, applied in the context of trading. I will touch on concepts that, at first, may seem very deep, scientific and even philosophical, but I will explain them in a simple and practical way so that you can have the necessary context. These concepts are based on the book Transurfing by Vadim Zeland. Next, we will review and polish the content to make it clearer and more fluid, giving you tools to understand how you can apply these concepts to your life as a trader and achieve a state of balance and efficiency in the financial environment.

Let's start by talking about the "space of variants," one of the key concepts of Vadim Zeland's Transurfing, which is still one of my favorite books. This concept is fascinating because it gives us a different perspective on how probabilities and fate work. It's a very similar idea to some theories of quantum physics that are being explored in the scientific field. Imagine that all possibilities exist, at the same time, in an infinite field of variants.

Each decision we make leads us to one of those probabilities, but the rest of the options don't disappear, but remain in that field of variants as latent possibilities. It's like the theory of "parallel universes" or the "many world's interpretation" (multiverse) that Hugh Everett proposed in 1957. In that theory, there are multiple parallel realities that result from different decisions or events. What we live is just one of those infinite probabilities.

To understand this better, let's think about the famous Double Slit Experiment, performed by Thomas Young in 1801 and later applied to quantum mechanics. This experiment showed that particles, such as electrons, can behave either as particles or as waves. When there is no observer, particles pass through both slits and generate interference patterns, suggesting that they are existing in multiple states at once. But if we notice them, those particles collapse into a single state, indicating that our observation directly influences the outcome. This is also how the space of variants works: all possibilities are there, but what we experience depends on our attention and emotional energy. What we focus our energy on is what collapses and manifests in our reality.

The central idea here is that our reality is not predetermined or fixed, but is in a constant state of potentiality, waiting for us to observe and choose it. In the context of Transurfing, we are taught to direct our energy consciously to manifest the reality we wish to experience, and this is achieved by staying calm and avoiding emotional burnout in situations that upset us. The key is to learn to choose, and not simply react to circumstances.

You're probably wondering: what does this have to do with trading? Well, every trade we make is like that double-slit experiment. If we remain calm and emotionally detached, there are multiple possible outcomes for every trade. But if we focus too much on a specific outcome, especially if our emotions are influenced by fear or expectations, what we're doing is collapsing that reality negatively.

Our emotions, especially negative ones like fear, anxiety or greed, act as the interfering observer, causing the outcome to end up being unfavorable. On the other hand, when we operate from a state of calm and stability, without being attached to the outcome, we allow the best possible variant to manifest because we are aligned with the natural flow of the financial system.

The financial environment, with its chaotic and unpredictable nature, behaves like a quantum system full of probabilities. Every move within this realm can be seen as a new fork in the space of variants, creating different possible trajectories. In this sense, our attitude and emotions are like the observer that decides which of these variants will manifest itself. If we face fear when prices fall, we might eliminate the possibility of an unfavorable outcome by hastily closing positions. If we let ourselves be carried away by greed, we might ignore important signals and end up losing. But if we manage to maintain a state of balance and mental clarity, without being carried away by impulses, we can choose the best variant available.

This concept also invites us to reflect on the power of intention in trading. When we enter into a trade with a clear intention and stay focused on it, without allowing negative emotions to cloud our judgment, we are actually aligning ourselves with the variant we want to manifest. Intention is like a compass that guides us through the space of variants, and when that intention is firm and free of emotional baggage, we are more likely to achieve the outcome we desire. On the other hand, this does not mean that we can control the financial environment; it means that we can control how we respond to it, and in that way, influence the variant that manifests for us.

Ultimately, Transurfing and the concept of field of options teach us that we have more power over our reality than we think. It's not about fighting against the conditions of the environment or trying to predict them, but about learning to flow with them, to consciously choose our reactions and to maintain a clear and detached intention. In doing so, we become conscious observers who have the ability to choose the best possible variant in every situation, both in trading and in life.

The Crash of 1929 was one of the most devastating financial events in history. It all started with a huge euphoria in the stock market, where people borrowed to invest and stocks rose out of control. In October of the same year, the bubble began to deflate. Fear gripped investors, and this unleashed a massive wave of sales that sank the financial system. Within days, the value of shares plummeted, causing a total collapse in financial confidence. It was a moment where euphoria quickly turned to panic, and millions of people saw their investments disappear overnight.

Banks closed, businesses went bankrupt, and unemployment skyrocketed. This cycle shows how collective fear can create a domino effect:

everyone sold for fear that prices would continue to fall, and this panic-fueled sell-off amplified the fall and led to a spiral of financial destruction. The lack of confidence spread rapidly, causing even the most solid sectors to succumb to the pressure. The situation continued to worsen, and more and more people and companies were dragged into this widespread collapse.

This event not only ruined the American economy, but also had a global impact, giving rise to the Great Depression, a decade marked by poverty and mass unemployment. From a Transurfing perspective, it was an example of how the energy of collective panic attracted the worst possible reality, turning a correction in the financial sphere into a crisis of historic proportions.

More recently, we can observe the impact of collective fear during the financial asset crash in March 2020 due to the COVID-19 pandemic. Uncertainty and the effects of the virus on the global economy led to a massive sell-off of assets. Within weeks, major stock indices suffered historic declines, and volatility reached levels never seen before. From a Transurfing perspective, the collective energy of fear and uncertainty collapsed reality into a negative scenario. Despite this, we could also see how, over time, the financial environment began to recover as confidence was restored, demonstrating how the shift in emotional energy can alter the course of events.

Another recent example is the cryptocurrency crash in late 2021 and early 2022. After a period of great euphoria and exponential growth, fear of regulations, rising interest rates, and other macroeconomic factors triggered a sell-off in the crypto world. Prices of assets like Bitcoin and Ethereum fell sharply, and many novice investors were swept up in the collective panic, selling at the worst possible time. This is another example of how collective energy, in this case fear and uncertainty, can influence financial behavior and lead to a negative variant crash.

Quantum Superposition and Trading

The superposition principle in quantum physics states that a particle can be in several states at once, until someone observes it and "collapses" it into one. Erwin Schrödinger illustrated this concept with his Schrödinger's cat thought experiment: a cat in a box can be both alive and dead at the same time, until the box is opened and its state observed. This seemingly abstract concept has direct implications in many areas of our lives, including trading, where every decision we make can be understood as a superposition of possible outcomes.

In trading, every decision we make works similarly to quantum superposition: as long as we don't know the outcome of a trade, it remains in a state of dual possibility, being both a potential success and a potential failure. That is, as long as the trade is still open, and the outcome has not yet manifested, there is a superposition of probabilities until we decide to close it. How we interact with that possibility, our emotions and our mindset, will determine which of those states materializes and what kind of reality we will collapse into.

If we operate from a state of balance, with a clear and detached mindset, we contribute to collapsing the most favorable variant. If, on the other hand, we let fear or greed influence our decisions, we collapse a less desirable variant, often harming our financial interests. This metaphor of quantum superposition and the collapse of possibilities invites us to reflect on the role our emotions play and how they directly affect the results we obtain in the financial environment.

Trading with emotional detachment is essential to staying on the path to success. Richard Dennis, the legendary trader, taught the "Turtle Traders" that to be successful, it was essential to remain detached and follow a plan, without being carried away by emotions. The Turtle Traders were a group of people who, under Dennis' guidance, learned to apply a trading system based on clear rules and rigorous discipline. Many of them had no prior experience in the financial field, but they achieved impressive results by following this structured approach. Dennis taught them that the secret to trading success was not in accurately predicting every move in the financial system, but in following the plan with rigor, discipline and without being affected by the emotions of the moment.

This disciplined approach allowed them to trade effectively even in highly volatile situations, showing that emotional detachment and discipline are essential to weathering favorable variations. Price volatility, which can trigger intense emotional reactions such as fear or greed, becomes a constant test for traders.

Those who manage to remain calm and operate from a clear and disciplined state of mind can take advantage of the opportunities that present themselves during these moments of chaos, while those who act on emotional impulses often end up making detrimental decisions.

We can learn from more recent events, such as the volatility in the financial environment during 2022, when inflation and global monetary policy began to affect asset prices. At that time, markets were shaken by fears of interest rate hikes and the impact on the global economy, leading to a significant decline in stock indices.

This context of uncertainty and fear led many investors to make hasty decisions, selling their assets in panic and taking considerable losses. However, those investors who managed to hold their ground, avoid hasty decisions and maintain a long-term mindset found valuable opportunities to enter the market at lower prices, once the situation began to stabilize.

This example shows that calmness and patience allow us to see opportunities when everyone else is caught up in panic. Just as quantum physicists discuss the superposition of states, traders must acquire skills to examine all probabilities without allowing collective fear to lead us to collapse the negative variant.

For a trader, emotional balance is as important as technical skill; the ability to remain calm and stick to a well-defined plan is what makes the difference between success and failure.

The overlay also teaches us that possibilities are open until the very last moment. That means that every trade can be successful or unsuccessful, and our role as traders is to observe without negatively interfering with emotions such as fear or anxiety. Maintaining a neutral state of mind, without expectations or attachments, allows the financial system to move according to its own dynamics, and we can act objectively. When a trader observes financial movements in a detached manner, he can respond rather than react, and this is crucial to collapsing the most favorable variant.

Another important aspect to consider is how superposition can be applied to planning our trading strategies. Every strategy we develop has multiple potential outcomes. How we apply it, the decisions we make, and our ability to follow the plan will determine which of those outcomes will manifest. Similar to how observation collapses a quantum state, our actions and decisions as investors determine the outcome of our strategy. That's why mental clarity and confidence in our strategy are critical to manifesting the best possible outcomes.

A key lesson from the superposition principle in trading is that we must be open to all probabilities without clinging to a single expected outcome. Financial reality is constantly changing, and what may seem like a loss at one point can turn into an opportunity later on. Those traders who manage to take a broad, detached view, without getting caught up in specific expectations, are the ones who have the greatest chance of long-term success. This doesn't mean we shouldn't have clear goals, but rather that we must be flexible and adaptive in the face of the uncertain and changing nature of the financial system.

Furthermore, it is important to note that, just like in quantum physics, the energy we bring to our decisions affects the outcome. If we operate with a fear or scarcity mindset, we are likely to end up collapsing an unfavorable variant. On the contrary, if we operate with confidence, following a well-structured plan and with a clear vision of our objectives, we are bringing positive energy that increases our chances of success. Trading is a reflection of our internal state, and the quality of our decisions is directly related to our ability to stay balanced.

The principle of superposition offers us a powerful metaphor for understanding how our emotions and decisions affect our trading in the financial environment. The key for investors is to learn to maintain a state of emotional stability, to observe all possibilities without collapsing negative variants driven by fear or greed, and to act with discipline and detachment. Only in this way can we collapse the most favorable variant and achieve success in trading.

The ability to observe financial movements objectively, without emotional interference, allows us to act with clarity and take advantage of the opportunities that arise, even in the midst of chaos. Superposition and trading are deeply connected, and understanding this connection gives us a significant advantage in our journey as traders.

Excessive potential and its influence

Vadim Zeland talks about the concept of "excessive potential" in Transurfing. This occurs when we give too much importance to something, creating an energetic imbalance that attracts balancing forces that often act against us. Excessive potential manifests when we become obsessed with a specific outcome or try to force the financial system to go in the direction we want. This creates an internal tension that prevents us from making objective decisions and, consequently, leads to unfavorable results.

Excessive potential arises from an attachment mindset, when we attribute too much importance to a single event or outcome. Instead of allowing the financial environment to flow and react calmly, we try to exert excessive control, which generates an excess of energy focused on a single point.

This excess attracts what Zeland calls "balancing forces," whose function is to restore balance, often in a way that is detrimental to us. The greater the level of importance we attribute to an outcome, the more energy we generate, thereby increasing the likelihood of triggering adverse effects.

A famous example of excessive potential is the case of Nick Leeson, the trader who led to the collapse of Barings Bank in the 1990s. Leeson took huge risks, convinced that he could manipulate the financial system in his favor and recover from initial losses. His obsession with winning and avoiding failure created huge excess potential, and the balancing forces eventually caught up with him, causing the bank to collapse.

This case demonstrates that obsessive focus and an inability to accept losses can be extremely damaging, even in the financial world. Leeson not only lost money, but lost control over his own decisions, allowing excess potential to dominate his every action.

Something similar happened during the cryptocurrency boom in 2017. Many people, motivated by the fear of missing out (the famous "FOMO"), became obsessed with the idea of making quick profits. This collective desire generated enormous excess potential. The vast majority of novice investors jumped into the market without a proper understanding of the risks involved, driven only by the promise of rapid and spectacular returns. When prices eventually corrected, those who lost the most were those who clung to the outcome without considering the possibility of a significant correction.

This correction was the manifestation of the balancing forces that restored equilibrium, and the excess potential created an imbalance that inevitably corrected itself, usually in a way unfavorable to those who were most attached to the outcome.

We can see another example of over-leverage in the collapse of Archegos Capital Management in 2021. Founder Bill Hwang took extremely leveraged positions, betting heavily on certain stocks and believing that his strategy could only result in success. This belief and overconfidence created considerable over-leverage.

When the financial system did not respond as he expected, the balancing forces came into play, causing massive losses that led to the collapse of Archegos and generated a domino effect that affected several large banks. This event reminds us that even experienced investors can fall into the trap of over-leverage if they fail to maintain a balanced and detached mindset.

The lesson we can draw from the concept of excess potential is that in trading it is essential to maintain a balanced mindset. We should not put too much emphasis on a single trade or outcome, or attribute more importance to it than necessary. It is essential to remember that the financial environment is unpredictable, and the best way to navigate it is with a flexible and detached attitude. The importance of flexibility lies in our ability to adapt to the unexpected, without creating resistance or obsession, which allows us to flow with financial movements instead of fighting them.

Excessive potential can also manifest itself when we desperately try to avoid losses. This obsession with not losing, or the fear of failure, creates a great deal of internal tension and attracts balancing forces that can lead us to precisely the outcome we want to avoid. To avoid this imbalance, it is important to accept that losses are part of trading and that we cannot control everything. The real skill lies in knowing how to manage those losses rationally, without allowing them to affect our mindset. By accepting that we will not always win, we reduce the level of tension and avoid the creation of excessive potential that could act against us.

Another common manifestation of overpotential occurs when we set specific financial goals and stick to them intensely. While having goals is important, obsessing over achieving them at all costs can create an internal pressure that leads to impulsive and risky decisions.

A trader may feel obligated to meet a daily profit target, and when prices don't behave as expected, they will try to force trades to meet that target. This attitude creates overpotential that often results in losses. It's critical to set flexible goals and understand that the path to financial success is not always linear.

On the other hand, successful traders are those who know how to balance their emotions and do not get carried away by the obsession of winning or the fear of losing. Maintaining a detached mindset, accepting results without resistance, and acting according to a well-structured plan, allows one to trade effectively without generating excessive potential.

Discipline and patience are key to avoiding excessive attachment and maintaining the mental clarity necessary to make objective decisions. By decreasing internal tension and avoiding emotional attachment, the likelihood of balancing forces acting against us is reduced.

Strategies to Avoid Excessive Potential

A positive example of how to avoid overpotential is the approach of traders who follow systematic investment strategies, such as algorithmic or quantitative trading. These investors develop specific rules for entering and exiting positions and strictly adhere to them, without involving emotions in the process.

By relying on a predefined system, they reduce the likelihood of creating overpotential and thus avoid attracting unfavorable balancing forces. This approach allows them to operate with a more objective and less reactive mindset, which is essential for long-term success.

Another strategy to avoid excessive potential is to practice effective risk management. Using tools such as stop losses and managing position size helps limit losses and maintain a reasonable level of exposure to the market.

By having a clear risk management plan, traders can trade with greater confidence and without the constant fear of losing large sums of money. This reduces internal tension and prevents excessive potential from being generated that can destabilize their decisions.

Practicing mindfulness can also be helpful in avoiding excessive potential. By developing greater awareness of our thoughts and emotions, we can detect when we are starting to obsess over an outcome or when we are creating too much importance around a trade. This awareness allows us to step back, re-evaluate our situation, and adjust our approach before excessive potential becomes a problem.

The concept of excess potential teaches us that attachment and obsession with an outcome can be our worst enemies in trading. Learning to let go, to accept what happens and to operate without unnecessary tension, helps us to stay balanced and increases our chances of success in the market. Instead of generating excess energy around our operations, we must learn to flow with the market, observing and responding calmly, which allows us to collapse the most favorable variants without attracting balancing forces against us. Maintaining an attitude of detachment, setting flexible goals and practicing good risk management are fundamental tools to reduce excess potential and operate in a more effective and balanced way.

The Observer and the Collapse of Reality

In quantum mechanics, the role of the observer is crucial to understanding how reality manifests. The Double Slit experiment revealed that quantum particles exist in a state of superposition until an observer intervenes, at which point they collapse into a single reality. This phenomenon, known as the collapse of the wave function, is a clear demonstration that reality is neither fixed nor absolute, but depends on conscious observation. This concept is fundamental to Transurfing and has profound implications for trading.

Every trader is a quantum observer in the financial environment. Our emotions, thoughts, and expectations act as the "observer" that determines which of the many possible variants will manifest in a trade. If an investor operates from a place of calm and detachment, he or she is more likely to collapse favorable variants. However, if an investor is caught up in fear, anxiety, or the desire to control financial movements, these emotions are reflected in the results of his or her trades, collapsing less desirable variants.

The act of observing is not neutral; our expectations directly influence the reality we experience. This implies that the investor's mental state is crucial in determining the results he or she will obtain, and working on maintaining emotional clarity becomes a key priority.

When traders act from a place of calm and objectivity, they are essentially tuning into the best possible version of events in the financial environment. The mindset with which one views opportunities makes the difference between generating positive results or getting caught in cycles of loss. The ability to maintain a balanced and conscious state of mind allows investors to be able to navigate complex situations without succumbing to pressure, which ultimately determines whether a favorable variant collapses or not.

One of the most famous traders in history, Jesse Livermore, who traded on the New York Stock Exchange in the early 20th century, understood the role of the observer in trading perfectly. Livermore knew that the financial environment was full of possibilities and that his success depended on his ability to observe without becoming attached to immediate results.

During the financial panic of 1907, Livermore observed the system from a place of calm, while many other investors collapsed their variants in losses due to panic. By keeping a clear mind and observing patiently, Livermore was able to take advantage of the crash and generate one of his greatest fortunes. This is a perfect example of how emotional control and the ability to observe without reacting automatically can lead to extraordinary results.

Jesse Livermore not only showed how calmness could lead to success, but also how emotional attachment can be a trader's worst enemy. At various points in his life, Livermore experienced ups and downs that took him from riches to bankruptcy. These episodes also illustrate how the role of the observer can be both a source of success and failure, depending on the state of mind.

When he was carried away by emotions, he collapsed unfavorable variants, which led to huge losses. This highlights the importance of cultivating a constant mindset of detachment to prevent negative emotions from influencing the observation process.

Another notable trader who understood the role of the observer was Paul Tudor Jones, who became known for predicting and profiting from the 1987 financial market meltdown known as "Black Monday." Jones saw early signs of a correction and acted with a disciplined plan, while most participants panicked. By observing from a calm, detached perspective, Jones was able to make decisions that allowed him to protect his capital and make significant profits at a time when other traders were suffering large losses. This example underscores how conscious, detached observation can lead to success even in the worst of circumstances.

The collapse of reality in trading is also reflected in the behavior of the masses. When large groups of investors are carried away by collective emotions, such as panic or euphoria, they tend to collapse variants that reflect those emotions. This is evident in the booms and busts of the financial sphere, or better known today in the world of cryptocurrencies as pumps and dumps, where the behavior of the collective observer affects the direction of prices. A recent example is the financial crisis of 2008, where the collective fear of investors collapsed, variants of massive losses throughout the global system.

Traders who knew how to observe from a distance and did not get carried away by panic were able to identify valuable opportunities during the recovery. Staying calm and observing without entering the spiral of collective emotions is a skill that can make all the difference between success and failure.

Crowd behavior is particularly interesting when looking at the role of social media in shaping trends in the financial environment. Recently, we have seen how communities on platforms like Reddit and Twitter (currently called X) can affect prices through focused collective observation, as was the case with the GameStop short squeeze in 2021.

The coordinated action of millions of small investors collapsed an unexpected variant, creating a spectacular surge in the GameStop stock price. This event demonstrates how the power of collective observation, motivated by a common feeling, can change financial reality in a drastic way. On the other hand, it also shows how collective euphoria can result in losses for those who join the movement without a solid plan, ultimately collapsing unfavorable variants for many.

Mind control and the collapse of favorable variants

This concept is also supported by several authors, such as Brian Tracy, who emphasizes the importance of mental and emotional control in decision-making. Tracy states that success in any field depends largely on our ability to observe the facts without being swept away by negative emotions. The more control we have over our emotions, the more favorable the variants we attract into our life. This means that we must constantly work on our internal state, cultivating a mindset that is aligned with mental balance and detachment, which will allow us to collapse variants that are in our favor.

For a trader, being a good observer involves more than just analyzing charts or following technical indicators. It means cultivating a calm and detached attitude toward outcomes. Successful traders do not allow fear or greed to influence their decisions. Instead, they keep a clear mind and observe the facts as they are, without projecting their own expectations or fears onto them. This type of conscious observation is what allows them to collapse favorable variants and achieve sustained success in the economic context.

The key is to develop the skill of being a conscious observer. The more aware we are of our thoughts and emotions, the more we can influence the reality we are creating. This means learning to observe the economic context and our own reactions, without allowing our emotions to cloud our judgment. In doing so, we become true masters of our economic reality, able to consciously choose the best possible variants. This level of awareness also allows us to identify patterns of behavior that may be negatively affecting our decisions and make the necessary adjustments to improve our operations.

A practical tool for developing mindfulness is meditation. Meditation helps to calm the mind and create a space between our emotions and our decisions, which is essential in trading. By meditating regularly, traders can learn to keep a clear and detached mind, allowing them to observe the economic context without reacting impulsively. This contributes to collapsing more favorable variants, as decisions made from a calm state are much more effective than those motivated by fear or greed.

Another important strategy is visualization. Visualizing success and desired outcomes can help traders focus their observation on favorable variants. By visualizing a positive outcome with details, the trader is essentially training his or her mind to tune into those variants and draw them into reality. Visualization, combined with disciplined action, can be a powerful tool to influence outcomes and collapse beneficial variants.

The role of the observer in trading is essential to determining the results we obtain. Maintaining a conscious, calm and detached attitude allows us to positively influence the variables that we collapse in the economic context. Emotional control, detachment and the cultivation of a conscious mindset are fundamental tools to ensure that our observations align with the best possible results.

Whether through meditation, visualization or affirmations, developing a capacity for conscious observation makes us true architects of our economic reality. In the economic context, as in life, the way we observe determines what we experience. Being a conscious observer, with the ability to remain detached from negative emotions and focused on opportunities, is the key to achieving sustained success trading in the financial arena.

Transurfing's concept of field of options invites us to reflect on the flexible nature of reality and the active role we play in creating our experiences, both in life and in trading. As we have seen, economic realms are not a static entity; they are constantly changing, and our decisions, emotions, and expectations determine which version of reality we experience. Every trade we open, every analysis we perform, is a choice that connects us to a specific variant of the future.

Trading, like quantum mechanics, confronts us with an infinite sea of possibilities, where the outcome depends on both our conscious decisions and our internal vibration. What Transurfing teaches us is that we do not need to force the economic context or create opportunities from scratch; instead, we must learn to tune into the right variants, those that already exist and are aligned with our internal state. For traders, this is a powerful message, as it reminds them that their success does not depend solely on their technical knowledge, but on their ability to manage their emotions and operate from a place of balance and detachment.

Furthermore, we must remember that just as the quantum universe is full of variations, the economic context is also full of opportunities. We do not need to obsess over a single operation or a single outcome. Variations are always present, and our task is to maintain a state of mind that allows us to access those that favor us.

Detachment is not indifference, but the ability to act from a position of clarity, without the weight of expectations clouding our vision. This approach will help us not only to succeed, but also to enjoy the process, to learn from each experience, and to grow both personally and professionally.

At this point, I want to clarify that although these concepts may seem esoteric, they are actually deeply connected to scientific principles. My goal is to offer you a different perspective, which can help you better understand life and the universe, as well as apply this knowledge practically in trading.

Chapter II

Pendulums in Trading

From the moment we begin to learn about economics, we are taught to follow the opinions of "experts," to obey the signals of institutions, to listen to the news and to act according to the prevailing trend. This mentality makes us followers of market pendulums, such as trends, expert analysis and collective feelings of fear or euphoria. Without realizing it, we fall under the influence of these forces that condition our decisions and bind us to their energetic dynamics.

In the trading world, pendulums are collective forces created when many traders and investors direct their thoughts and emotions in the same direction. These forces can have a significant impact on the behavior of the economic environment, and we often don't even realize how they influence our decisions. Just like in our daily lives, these energies act independently, subjecting traders to their own rules. So how can we be aware of this manipulation and avoid falling into its traps?

Vadim Zeland, the creator of the concept of pendulums in Transurfing, explains that these structures feed off our mental and emotional energy. In the economic context, a pendulum is formed when many participants align emotionally, creating a force that influences the decisions of all involved. In this way, emotional patterns can lead us to act impulsively and unconsciously, harming our interests.

In trading, these destructive energies manifest themselves in collective emotions such as panic during a crash, which leads to a sell-off, or uncontrolled greed during a speculative bubble, when many invest without critical reflection or foundation. These pendulums feed on our overflowing emotions and our desire to belong to the flow, keeping us trapped and distancing us from the objectivity we need to trade successfully.

Emotional patterns feed into mass behavior. When many traders follow an uptrend unquestionably, believing that prices will continue to rise forever, a collective movement is created that amplifies that trend. However, when this pendulum loses its force, the collapse can be devastating for those who follow it without critical analysis. For example, during the dotcom bubble in the late 1990s, the pendulum of technological euphoria led many investors to make irrational decisions, only to see their assets lose value massively when the bubble burst.

Another manifestation of destructive emotional patterns occurs when investors are influenced by social pressure and the fear of missing out, known as FOMO (Fear Of Missing Out). This fear can lead to hasty and ill-informed decisions, which often result in significant losses. Friedrich Nietzsche spoke about the importance of avoiding being part of the herd and thinking independently, and this advice is especially relevant in the world of trading, where pendulums constantly try to drag traders towards collective decisions that are not always the best.

Carl Jung also noted that the collective unconscious tends to create group dynamics that can lead to self-destructive behavior if left unattended. This manifests when traders fall into cycles of impulsive behavior and automatic reactions to news, without stopping to think whether these actions are aligned with their personal goals. This is one of the reasons why many investors fail: they act under the influence of these energies, not realizing that their decisions are being manipulated by the collective energy.

Quantum physics, with its concept of entanglement, provides a good parallel. Quantum entanglement suggests that two particles can be connected in such a way that the state of one instantly affects the state of the other, regardless of the distance. Similarly, the thoughts and emotions of operators become entangled, creating a resonance that gives rise to the emotional patterns of the economic realm. Carl Jung also spoke of a similar connection, referring to the collective unconscious, where shared emotions and thoughts create patterns of behavior that affect the whole of society, including the economic realm.

Jung developed the concept of the collective unconscious, a part of our psyche that contains the shared experiences of humanity, with archetypes and patterns of behavior common to all. In trading, the collective unconscious manifests itself when investors act in similar ways due to shared emotions and expectations.

When the majority feels fear of a possible downturn, this feeling becomes a collective force that drives many to sell, creating a downward spiral. It is the collective unconscious in action. In the same way, general enthusiasm during a bubble can lead to irrational overbuying, causing many traders to follow the trend without critical analysis. Jung believed that by becoming aware of these patterns, we could free ourselves from their influence. This means recognizing when we are being pulled by the collective unconscious and, instead of acting automatically, making decisions based on objective analysis and our own strategy.

We can see examples of this in everyday life, such as the phenomenon of panic buying during an economic crisis. When a group of people start hoarding certain goods out of fear of a shortage, this action spreads to others, even those who originally had no intention of doing so. Thus, the collective unconscious becomes a collective movement that drags the majority towards irrational behavior. Traders, acting under the influence of the collective unconscious, end up moving en masse and increasing volatility. The key to avoiding this is to recognize these patterns and maintain a critical and conscious mindset.

Pendulums can be "constructive" or destructive, but in the context of trading, we usually mention destructive pendulums that divert investors from their personal goals.

In everyday life, emotional patterns are present in many areas. A clear example is fashion: when a trend becomes popular, most people follow it without questioning whether they really like it or whether it benefits them. Another example is the work environment in a company: when the majority of employees adopt a certain attitude, whether optimistic or pessimistic, that energy becomes a pendulum that influences the general atmosphere of the workplace. Even in politics, these energies manifest themselves when the speeches of certain leaders manage to attract large masses of followers, who adopt their ideas and act without critical reflection.

In trading, emotional patterns appear in the form of economic trends, whether in bullish or bearish phases. Traders, by joining these currents without their own analysis, are feeding the pendulum and allowing its influence to grow. For example, when a stock or cryptocurrency begins to rise rapidly in price, many feel the urge to buy, creating a collective movement of euphoria that can lead to the formation of speculative bubbles. On the other hand, during a fall, the pendulum of fear leads many investors to sell at the worst possible moment, without considering whether the fall is temporary or whether there are really fundamental reasons to do so.

The key to freeing ourselves from destructive pendulums is to be aware of their existence and make decisions based on objective analysis. Understanding that our emotions and those of other participants often drag us in directions that are not necessarily the best for our interests allows us to distance ourselves and act more rationally.

Let's talk a little more in-depth about what lies behind pendulums in the economic sphere because it is a really worth concept understanding well. A pendulum in the economic context is created when the mental energies of a group of operators is aligned, that is, when the thoughts and emotions of many people go in the same direction. This energetic synchronization generates a structure that acts as an autonomous force, a kind of invisible entity that begins to influence those who are connected to it, often without us realizing it.

Think of it this way: Imagine a group of people in a room, all very excited, talking about the next big cryptocurrency. At first, some are enthusiastic, others are a bit more skeptical, but slowly, the enthusiasm starts to spread. Eventually, the majority is convinced that this cryptocurrency will be the next big opportunity to get rich. What has happened here is that a pendulum has been created: the collective energy of that group has aligned, and now that enthusiasm has a life of its own and continues to drive people to act on that collective feeling.

This phenomenon can be clearly seen in the formation of an economic trend or when a new "meme" cryptocurrency emerges. Traders, observing a trend, tend to emotionally align themselves with it. If they feel fear of missing out (what we know as FOMO) or panic about losing more money (the famous FUD - Fear, Uncertainty and Doubt), that accumulated energy starts to feed the collective force. This is how the pendulum gains strength and becomes a kind of invisible force that controls those who operate within its frequency.

Economic spheres, in theory, operate because of supply and demand, but these are greatly influenced by collective psychology. When investors allow their decisions to be dictated by fear or greed, they are acting under the influence of destructive pendulums. When the economic context experiences a sudden fall and panic spreads, many traders sell without analyzing the situation rationally. This behavior is the result of the energy that has built up in the collective force of panic. The more investors contribute to this energy, the greater the movement in that direction, and that is why we can see such abrupt falls.

Vadim Zeland describes these energies as independent structures that seek to perpetuate their existence by feeding off the energy of individuals. So when the panic pendulum takes over, it becomes extremely difficult for traders to act logically and calmly. It's a bit like trying to stay calm in the middle of a stampede – you get swept away by the collective momentum.

Viktor Frankl, a psychologist and Holocaust survivor, spoke about the importance of finding an inner purpose and not being swept away by external forces. In the context of trading, this means not succumbing to the energy of the pendulums of the economic realm, staying calm and following a strategy that is based on principles and rational analysis.

One of the most difficult challenges in trading is precisely staying aware of when we are being swept away by a collective movement. The key to overcoming this challenge is to be present, critical, and not mindlessly get carried away by the wave. Instead of succumbing to FOMO or general panic, we need to make decisions that are aligned with our goals and based on well-founded analysis. The next time you are faced with a volatile economic situation, ask yourself: "Am I making this decision because it is what my analysis tells, or simply because I feel that everyone else is doing it?" This simple question can help you identify if you are under the influence of a pendulum and allow you to regain control of your decisions.

And now I want us to pause for a moment to talk about a fundamental aspect of destructive pendulums: their constant battle for dominance. These energies, as collective forces seeking to prevail, are in a constant struggle to attract more supporters and fuel their oscillations. This competition generates a very evident effect in economic spheres, where different emotional forces try to impose themselves on each other, dragging operators into their dynamics. At the end of the day, emotional patterns do not just want to survive, they want to grow and strengthen themselves at the expense of the energy of their followers.

For example, when an uptrend begins to form, the pendulum of euphoria and greed tries to attract as many investors as possible. This leads many traders to enter the market convinced that prices will continue to rise, without critically analyzing whether the asset is really worth it. Conversely, when the environment begins to fall, the collective force of fear takes over, dragging many investors into a massive sell-off, usually at the worst possible time. In both cases, traders believe they are making rational decisions, when in reality they are being dragged along by these collective forces that seek to perpetuate themselves.

To illustrate this differently, let's think about fashion. When a piece of clothing or style becomes popular, many people jump on the trend, even without questioning whether they really like it or whether it suits them. This is the pendulum of fashion, which grows with each new follower who decides to adopt that piece of clothing.

Then, when the pendulum loses strength, that same fashion becomes obsolete, and people get rid of it almost immediately, without stopping to think about why they adopted it in the first place. The same thing happens in trading: investors tend to follow trends without any analysis of their own, and then abandon those positions as soon as the context changes, without questioning whether their decision was correct or not.

In the economic realm, besides collective emotion, there are other tools and signals that feed the pendulums, such as technical indicators and transaction volume analysis. When transaction volumes increase and the price seems to confirm a trend, many retail traders feel the urge to enter the dynamics so as not to miss out on the opportunity, which feeds the collective force of FOMO (fear of missing out).

Furthermore, when important public figures, such as Elon Musk, mention a cryptocurrency on social media, they can trigger massive price movements. Here we see how a simple message can fuel or weaken a collective movement, creating a constant battle for investors' attention and energy.

Another example of the battle of these energies is the competition between traditional assets and cryptocurrencies. The emotional patterns of traditional assets, such as stocks and bonds, try to discredit the pendulums of cryptocurrencies, and vice versa. The media, economic analysts and important figures in the sector constantly present arguments that try to strengthen their side and attract more supporters. The intention is clear: to strengthen their own pendulum at the expense of the other.

For a conscious trader, it is essential to learn to identify these battles and not get caught up in them. Maintaining an independent perspective, critically analyzing the information and asking yourself if you are deciding out of your own conviction or because you are being carried away by the pendulum is the key to avoid falling victim to these swings. The best strategy is often to stay calm, take a step back and evaluate whether your decisions are aligned with your own goals and not with the emotions that predominate in the economic sphere at that moment.

How destructive pendulums influence trading

This market energy does not care about the well-being of individual traders. Its only intention is to keep moving, feeding off the energy generated by our emotions: fear, greed, desperation. And the more intense the emotion, the stronger the energy investors give to these pendulums.

This translates into extreme movements in the financial environment, such as collapses or irrational euphoria, where objectivity is lost. In this way, the destructive nature of these energies manifests itself when they drag traders into making decisions based on the behavior of the crowd, rather than based on conscious and rational analysis.

Let's take a more recent example: the collapse of Terra/Luna in the cryptocurrency market. This case is a clear example of how a destructive pendulum can influence thousands of investors. At first, the project created a collective movement of overwhelming optimism. Everyone wanted to be part of the next success, a feeling that was fueled through social media, recommendations from supposed experts, and the promise of extraordinary returns.

But when the first signs of trouble began, the collective force of fear took over, causing a stampede of sales and a sharp decline in the value of Terra/Luna. Traders who had previously been swept away by the euphoria of the pendulum now found themselves caught up in the pendulum of panic, losing a large part of their investments.

But it is not only these drastic events that reflect the destructive nature of this energy. There is a less obvious, but equally powerful aspect of how emotional patterns influence the structure of the financial system through technical elements. Let us think about technical indicators: many times, tools such as moving averages, RSI or MACD become reference points shared by numerous investors.

If enough people observe a buy signal in the crossover of moving averages, for example, a collective movement is created that drives further demand. But when this movement fades and prices fail to meet expectations, traders react abruptly, creating a cascade of sales that still follows the pendulum patterns.

The same goes for trading volumes. When there is a sudden spike in volume, many perceive it as a sign that something big is happening. This behavior creates a snowball effect where investors follow the volume, fueling the movement without necessarily understanding what is behind that increase. This action, in itself, strengthens the collective force and makes it a determining factor in the behavior of financial dynamics.

On the other hand, we cannot ignore the enormous influence of social media. Nowadays, platforms such as Twitter or Reddit can be real catalysts for pendulum swings in the market. All it takes is for a well-known figure to make a remark about a stock or a cryptocurrency for the mass of traders to align in the same direction.

We saw this clearly with the case of GameStop, where a group on Reddit managed to shake financial institutions by simply coordinating their action through the networks. In these cases, the pendulum of euphoria can reach unprecedented levels, but the fall can also be just as abrupt, affecting mainly those who entered late and without a plan.

David Bohm, a physicist and philosopher, spoke of the importance of understanding the totality of a system, rather than focusing only on its parts. Bohm believed that the universe is an indivisible system, where everything is interconnected. According to him, if we only look at the individual parts of a system, we lose sight of how they interact with each other and how they form a coherent whole.

In his theory of the "implicate order," Bohm proposed that visible realities (the "explained order") emerge from a deeper level of reality that is hidden but connects them all. That is, what we see and perceive as real is only a superficial manifestation of a more fundamental order that underlies everything. This invites us to look beyond the obvious and try to understand the underlying connections that give rise to the manifestations we observe.

Applied to trading, this concept teaches us that we cannot limit ourselves to analyzing only individual movements in the financial environment, such as a stock price or a candlestick chart. We must try to see the whole picture and understand the underlying dynamics, hidden patterns and collective energies that affect market behavior. Bohm invites us to move away from a fragmented view to adopt a holistic perspective, understanding that every market movement is influenced by a complex web of interconnected factors, from investor psychology to global economic conditions.

In trading, understanding the whole allows us to identify those collective forces, or "pendulums," that influence the decisions of participants in the financial system. In this way, we can begin to see beyond the daily noise and understand how our own perception and action are being shaped by a broader, deeper reality. This helps us avoid being blindly swept away by the emotions of the market and instead make more conscious decisions aligned with a more comprehensive understanding of what is happening.

That's why it's essential to recognize when we're being influenced by a destructive market pendulum. If you notice that your decisions are being guided more by fear or collective euphoria than by detailed and objective analysis, you're probably under the influence of a collective movement. In these cases, the best strategy is to stop, take a step back, and reevaluate the situation from a place of calm and detachment. It's not about stopping using technical tools or ignoring the news, but about using them consciously, without falling into the trap of emotional patterns that seek to trap us.

How Great Traders Deal With Market Pendulums

I want us to think a little about how great traders deal with the invisible forces of the financial environment, the emotional patterns. This energy, these mass emotional movements that seem to drag us along, do not care about us as individuals. Their only intention is to keep oscillating, feeding off our emotions like fear and greed. But what do successful traders do in the face of this? Instead of letting themselves be carried away, they know how to recognize them and, many times, even how to use them to their advantage.

A good example of this is Paul Tudor Jones. This legendary trader understood early on that mass behavior is one of the greatest dangers in financial contexts. Paul knew that to be successful he had to act independently, moving away from the flow when necessary. It is not about doing the opposite just for the sake of defying the trend, but having the clarity to analyze for oneself and decide without getting carried away by the emotional tide. Imagine if everyone jumps into the water believing there is a treasure, but there is no one to ask if there really is something there or if it is worth the risk.

Warren Buffett is another perfect example of how to avoid the influence of pendulums. You've probably heard his famous quote: "Be fearful when others are greedy and greedy when others are fearful." That shows an in-depth understanding of how these collective energies work. When everyone is being swept up in the euphoria of a booming financial sector, Buffett knows it's time to step back and reevaluate. A prime example of how Buffett took advantage of the situation was during the 2008 financial crisis. While many investors were selling out of fear, he turned to investing in solid companies that were being unfairly punished by the panic in the financial environment. He bought shares of Goldman Sachs and General Electric at low prices, knowing that eventually these companies had intrinsic value that the financial environment was ignoring. That ability to stay out of the pendulum of collective panic allowed him to make huge profits.

Another interesting example is Stanley Druckenmiller, who has also been able to exploit weaknesses in financial systems. Druckenmiller worked alongside Soros and was instrumental in the famous bet against the pound.

But he has also demonstrated a great ability to anticipate movements in the financial environment, as he did during the technology bubble of the late 1990s. While many were carried away by the euphoria of technology stocks, Druckenmiller knew when to enter and, more importantly, when to exit before the energetic dynamic of enthusiasm collapsed. This ability to identify the moments when the pendulum is losing force and act accordingly has allowed him to achieve an impressive record of positive returns throughout his career.

But it's not all about challenging collective influences. Sometimes, the key is knowing how to flow. Lao-Tzu, the Chinese philosopher, said that wisdom consists of flowing like water, adapting without resistance to circumstances. This philosophy also has a direct application in trading. Great traders not only challenge the pendulum; they often also know how to adapt and wait for the right moment.

They know that the market is changing and that sometimes the best strategy is not to fight against the current, but to observe, wait, and act calmly. This ability to adapt and not react impulsively is what allows them to maintain the clarity to make effective decisions, even in times of high volatility.

Something that is also critical, and can be of great help to us retail investors, is learning to identify when our decisions are being guided by the crowd and when we are really following our own analysis. It is not easy; you have to be very honest with yourself and be willing to stop, step back and re-evaluate the situation. Great traders have learned to do this, not because they have supernatural abilities, but because they have practiced over and over again, developing the ability to recognize when they are being caught up in a collective movement.

So, the next time you see that everyone is acting in a certain way, ask yourself: does this make sense to me? Am I acting because I think it is the right thing to do, or because everyone else is doing it? Perhaps the key is to, like Buffett, be brave when everyone else is afraid, or like Soros, know when to take advantage of the weakness of the pendulum. But above all, the key is to remain clear and calm, without getting carried away by the current.

How to free yourself from destructive pendulums

To free ourselves from this destructive energy, it is essential to develop the ability to operate from a state of awareness and emotional detachment. This involves recognizing when our decisions are being influenced by fear, greed, or other collective emotions, and consciously deciding whether those decisions are really in our best interest. Here are some strategies to avoid falling under the influence of pendulums:

1. **Analyze objectively**: Before deciding, stop and ask yourself if you are acting on objective data or if you are reacting to the prevailing emotion in the financial environment. Objectivity is key to avoid being swept away by destructive emotional patterns. Make sure you evaluate relevant metrics, technical indicators and any other relevant data without being influenced by the noise of the financial system. The ability to analyze objectively will help

you identify when sector movements are being driven by emotional pendulums and when there are actually fundamentals behind them.

2. **Have a Clear Trading Plan**: A well-structured plan can help you avoid making impulsive decisions. Setting rules on when to enter and exit the market will allow you to trade more rationally, without falling under the influence of emotional patterns. Your trading plan should be aligned with your personal goals and not with the flow of the financial environment.

3. **Detaching from the results**: The key to freeing yourself from these energies is to trade from a state of emotional detachment. Understanding that each trade is just one of many possible variations, and that the outcome of a trade does not define your worth as a trader. You should not obsess over the success or failure of an individual trade, but rather focus on the process.

4. **Avoid sensational news**: News often amplifies the collective emotions of the financial system, creating an environment of fear or euphoria. Stay informed, but don't let sensationalism drag you into irrational decisions. The media often function as amplifiers of the sector's emotional patterns.

5. **Observe from a distance**: Imagine that you are an observer of the financial environment, rather than a participant. This perspective will help you see things more clearly and identify when a pendulum is forming that could lead you to wrong decisions. Observing from a distance will also allow you to avoid reacting impulsively to sudden movements in the financial system.

6. **Develop Emotional Resilience**: Emotional resilience is the ability to remain calm and mentally balanced, even in situations of uncertainty and volatility. To free yourself from destructive pendulums, it is crucial to strengthen your ability to manage stress and negative emotions. Meditation and mindfulness practice can be valuable tools to achieve this.

7. **Free yourself from the influence of the industry**: It is important to understand that fighting against a collective movement of the financial

environment only gives it more strength. For example, if a trader becomes obsessed with avoiding a loss and is constantly focused on what could go wrong, he is feeding that pendulum with his energy. The first rule to sinking a collective movement is to give up fighting it. The more we try to reject something that bothers us about the financial system, the more it haunts us. This translates into emotions such as frustration over a losing trade, fear of missing opportunities, or anger at the behavior of the industry.

Eckhart Tolle, author of The Power of Now, suggests that conscious presence is the best defense against external forces that seek to control our minds. In trading, this means being fully present in the moment of making decisions, without letting external noise or emotions divert you from your purpose. The ability to stay present and aware is critical to breaking free from destructive emotional patterns.

Pendulums are an inevitable part of the financial sector, and while we can't eliminate them, we can learn to recognize them and neutralize their influence on our decisions. As traders, we are not always aware of how collective emotions affect our decisions. But once we understand how these energies operate, we can take a step toward being conscious traders. And that is key because conscious trading is what allows us to act from a place of clarity and balance, and not from the automatic reaction that emotional patterns provoke.

Imagine that the financial field is like a great river, and these energies are the currents that drag you along. If you are not aware of them, they will take you wherever they want, without you being able to control it. But if you are aware, you can navigate that river with a purpose, avoiding the currents that do not suit you and taking advantage of those that do. Recognizing the pendulums does not mean fighting against them, but rather understanding how they act and how they affect our decisions, to then decide in a way that is more aligned with our individual goals.

A key part of becoming a conscious trader is learning to identify when you are under the influence of a pendulum. If you notice that you are making decisions out of fear of missing out on an opportunity or fear of losing what you already have, that is a clear sign that a collective movement is pulling you in. The same is true if you find yourself entering a trade because you see everyone talking about a specific stock or cryptocurrency, and you don't want to be left out. These are classic examples of how collective influences pull us in, and the first step to breaking free is to simply acknowledge their influence.

Trading consciously means not reacting automatically to collective emotions, but evaluating each situation from a state of calm and objectivity. How to achieve this? Well, a good strategy is to have a clear trading plan. When you have specific rules about when to enter and exit your investments, it is easier to avoid getting caught up in the euphoria or panic of the moment. Another way is to practice emotional detachment. Understanding that each trade is an opportunity to learn, and that the results, whether positive or negative, do not define your value as an investor.

A conscious trader also knows that his greatest strength is the ability to stand out from the crowd. It doesn't mean trading against the trend, but rather not being blindly swept along by it. As Warren Buffett said, "You must be fearful when others are greedy and greedy when others are fearful." This approach reminds us that, many times, true trading success comes from knowing how to stay calm when everyone around you is losing it.

Recognizing pendulums also involves observing how certain events, news, or even public figures can trigger a wave of collective emotions. The next time you see a sensational news story or a big rise or fall in the markets, take a moment to reflect. Are you reacting because there really are solid fundamentals, or are you being swept along with the current? This ability to question and critically analyze is what differentiates a conscious investor from one who simply follows the crowd.

Becoming a conscious trader is not something that is achieved overnight; it is a constant process of self-observation and learning. But every small step you take towards recognizing and releasing the influence of emotional patterns will bring you closer to consistent trading aligned with your goals. Remember, the financial world will always be full of pendulums trying to capture your attention and energy, but it is up to you whether you let yourself be carried away or choose to navigate your own path, consciously and with intention.

I want us to reflect together on something important: these energies are not only fed by those who blindly follow them, but also by those who try to fight against them. That is, whether you align yourself with the flow or attempt to resist it, your energy is being used by the pendulum. And this, in the world of trading, can have unexpected and not always positive consequences.

Imagine that the markets are falling, and the atmosphere is full of negative news. As a trader, you feel trapped in uncertainty and start experiencing fear and anxiety. If you make impulsive decisions by selling your positions, you not only lose money, but you are contributing to the strength of fear. That collective energy fuels the downward trend, creating a spiral where more and more traders are affected and act without rational analysis. The result: you fall into exactly what you wanted to avoid.

Financial pendulums can lead you to what you don't want. The more you focus on avoiding a negative situation, the more likely you are to end up facing it. Fear and resistance cause your energy to synchronize with the frequency of the pendulum, and that's when the worst expectations materialize. It's as if, by trying to escape from a problem, you're heading straight for it without realizing it.

A typical example is when an investor is obsessed with avoiding a significant loss. That constant worry, that excessive focus on not losing, ends up fixing his mental energy on the frequency of the fear pendulum. And what happens then? The trader gets carried away by emotion, sells at the worst possible moment and, in the end, materializes the loss he so wanted to avoid. The markets seem to almost respond to our deepest emotions, as if they mirror what we focus on.

To avoid this, the key is to maintain a conscious and detached stance in the face of financial fluctuations. Instead of fighting these energies, we must learn to observe them without getting emotionally involved. If there is negative information that does not directly affect our strategy or trading plan, the best decision is not to give it power, not to allow it to invade our mind and become a constant concern.

Let's think of an everyday example. Imagine it's raining and you don't want to get wet. The more you obsess about not getting wet, the more you notice every drop, every puddle, and you end up wetter than you would have been if you had simply accepted the rain and moved calmly. The same thing happens in trading: accepting the challenges of the financial environment and moving calmly will help you avoid being dragged by pendulums where you don't want to go.

In the financial context, this means that the more detached you are from collective emotions, the more you can make decisions from a rational place aligned with your goals. The conscious trader knows that markets will go up and down, that there will be gains and losses, but understands that their focus and energy should not be on avoiding every fall, but on following their plan with clarity and consistency. Freeing yourself from the influence of pendulums is essential to maintaining balance, minimizing losses, and, above all, operating from a place of calm and awareness.

Going with the Market: Sinking the Pendulum

In the world of trading, there is a crucial lesson that many are slow to learn: fighting market forces is actually feeding the very thing we want to avoid. If we try to confront financial movements directly, all we achieve is to give more strength to those forces that disturb us. This principle, known as the "pendulum swing," invites us to a wiser and more fluid approach: not to resist, but to accept and act with awareness.

Instead of fighting market forces, it is better to adopt a stance similar to aikido, the martial art, where the defender does not fight the attacker's force, but redirects it. When the financial environment hits us, we can learn to observe the movement, accompany that energy with a calm mind, and wait for the right moment to act without wasting our energy. This means accepting that markets can behave in unexpected ways and, instead of trying to change or confront them, understanding that such situations are part of their nature.

Imagine that the financial world is like an art gallery. There will be works that you like and others that simply don't connect with you, but there's no point in demanding that the ones you don't like be removed. You can choose to focus on those that do add value to your experience and, in the case of trading, choose strategies that allow you to maintain mental balance without reacting impulsively. Accepting the existence of those "paintings" that you don't like is the first step to stopping them from affecting you.

Being "empty" in front of the pendulum means not offering resistance, not giving anything that it can get caught on. It does not mean resignation, but rather observing from a calm position, acting from awareness and maintaining a neutral stance. When we do not react emotionally to a fall or an unexpected movement, the pendulum loses its power over us. For example, when the markets behave erratically and many traders react with anxiety, you can choose not to pass judgment or allow that energy to drag you down. This allows you to stay on a different frequency, from which you can make decisions with clarity.

A conscious trader knows that financial dynamics move according to their own rules, which are not under our control. Stopping fighting the system is the key to freeing up our energy and focusing on what we can control: our reaction. By acting from acceptance and not resistance, we manage to sink the pendulum and flow with the financial movements without getting caught in its destructive oscillations.

In some cases, ignoring or avoiding a collective movement may not be enough to free oneself from its influence. Sometimes, these collective forces are so persistent and dominant that simply "sagging" the energetic dynamic is not an option. So what can we do? We must find a different way to confront them, which we will call "extinguishing the pendulum."

Extinguishing a collective movement means acting in a way that does not feed the energy of that pendulum, but dissolves it. In the context of trading, it can be when trends seem to push in a specific direction, and you choose not to follow that flow, not from a reactive or resistant attitude, but from a position of detachment and serenity. In other words, it is about taking an unexpected action that breaks the cycle of the pendulum's energy.

Imagine a financial environment that is in a strong downtrend, and all traders are acting out of fear, selling mercilessly to avoid further losses. The force of fear has been endorsed by the vast majority. If you feel cornered by this pendulum and simply decide to react like everyone else, you are feeding it. But, if instead you decide to take a breath, analyze the real fundamentals, and realize that the fall is an overreaction without solid foundation, you might choose to hold your positions, or even buy more when prices are low. In this case, you are acting outside the script expected by the collective force of fear, extinguishing it for yourself.

A similar example can be seen when markets are in an uptrend and euphoria is dominating all investors. Prices are rising rapidly and there appears to be no ceiling in sight. In these situations, the influences of greed and enthusiasm can lead traders to buy at very high prices without analyzing the risks. Extinguishing the pendulum in this context means having enough discipline not to get carried away by euphoria and sell or at least not buy more when prices are irrational. It is acting cold-blooded when everyone is being dominated by greed.

The interesting thing about extinguishing a pendulum is that it doesn't always require dramatic or drastic action; sometimes the most effective action is simply not to react in the expected way. If the financial environment presents you with a situation that seems desperate, such as a big drop or a rise without clear foundations, and you manage not to react emotionally, you are extinguishing that pendulum. It's like being in an argument where the other person expects an intense reaction from you, but you choose to remain calm. By not responding with the expected energy, the force of the conflict dissolves.

A practical way to do this is to focus on the data and your trading plan rather than the emotions the system is trying to generate in you. When everyone is reacting to a news story extremely, you might ask yourself, "Does this news really change the fundamentals of my trading?" If the answer is no, then there is no reason to react. This way of acting breaks the cycle that the pendulum is trying to maintain.

Another technique that can help extinguish a collective movement is to change your perspective on what is happening. If financial conditions are behaving in a way that would normally irritate or make you nervous, endeavor to view it as a curious observer. Imagine that you are watching a movie, where the financial environment is the unpredictable protagonist. This allows you to distance yourself from the situation and act from a more focused place.

Remember, extinguishing a collective movement doesn't mean recklessly challenging the market or acting irrationally. It's about finding a way not to follow the script that the system and the pendulum are imposing, and acting from a place of balance and awareness. Sometimes the best way to extinguish a pendulum is to simply change the frequency of your thoughts and actions so that they don't match the pendulum's.

In short, pendulums exist because we give them energy, either through our emotional reaction or by acting in predictable ways. To extinguish a collective movement, we must break that feedback loop. Through calm, observation, and conscious actions, we can defuse the influence of these destructive energies and operate in ways that bring us closer to our goals, not those the system tries to impose on us.

Easy solutions to difficult problems

Often, in trading we face problems that seem to have no solution, which make us feel trapped in a cycle of frustration and despair. These problems can be a losing streak, an environment that does not behave as we expected, or simply the stress of not finding clear opportunities to trade. And this is where emotional patterns come in, those forces that, by focusing our attention negatively, keep us in a kind of labyrinth where everything seems more complicated than it really is.

The secret to finding easy solutions is to learn to "distance yourself" from the problem. Imagine you are in a room with several doors, but you can only see the wall in front of you. That wall is the problem, and the pendulums try to keep you looking only in that direction, to keep thinking there is no way out. But if you can relax and stop feeding the problem pendulum, you will be able to see the doors that were always there, waiting to be opened.

Let me be obvious: it is not easy to do so, and even less so when everything seems to be against you. But it is precisely in those moments that we need to stop immersing ourselves in the problem and start seeing the situation from a different perspective. This is what I call "taking a step back": acting as if you were an external observer, someone who is looking at the situation from the outside without getting emotionally involved. Instead of thinking "I have to solve this now, it is urgent," you can ask yourself: "What would be the easiest way to solve this if I were not rushing or under pressure?" Many times, the answer is simpler than we think, but the pendulum of the problem prevents us from seeing it.

Imagine you're going through a losing streak in your trading. It's easy to get into a state of frustration, where every new loss feels like confirmation that "everything is wrong." This mindset fixates your attention on the problem and keeps you stuck in a negative spiral. But if instead of focusing on how to get out of the maze, you decide to relax, take a break and observe calmly, perhaps you could see that the solution is not so complicated: you may just need to adjust your strategy, reduce the size of your positions, or even take a break to clear your mind.

The key here is to detach yourself from the problem and not let it consume you. By "stepping back," you allow yourself to see the situation with fresh eyes, and often the solution appears naturally. It's as if you stopped banging your head against the wall and simply turned around to see that there's a door right next door. The solution was always there, it's just that the pendulum kept you looking in the wrong direction.

Bruce Kovner is one of the most successful and respected traders in history. Founder of Caxton Associates, one of the most profitable investment firms in the world, Kovner was known for his ability to trade futures and currencies with an uncanny knack for managing risk. However, success was not always guaranteed, and one of his first great lessons came when he was just beginning his trading career.

In the 1970s, when Kovner was just getting started as a trader, he made a trade that nearly bankrupted him. He invested in soybean futures contracts with high confidence that the price would continue to rise. Initially, the trade was very successful, and soybean prices began to rise, earning him significant profits. At that point, Kovner felt invincible, just like many traders who will be carried away by a winning streak.

However, reality quickly changed. Soybean prices began to fall sharply due to unexpected news. Kovner, who had been emotionally reactive and panicked until then, was faced with the possibility of losing not only his profits but also his initial capital. That was when, instead of continuing to fuel the pendulum of fear, he decided to take a step back and "take some distance" from the situation.

Kovner forced himself out of the emotional trap he was experiencing. Instead of reacting impulsively and selling in the midst of the chaos, he decided to observe the situation calmly. He realized that selling at that moment would only have compounded his losses. He decided to hold his position with strict risk management, knowing that prices could stabilize. In the end, the trend reversed direction, and he was able to not only minimize his losses, but profit when prices recovered.

What Kovner learned at that time, and what separated him from most investors, was his ability to not get swept up in the collective emotions and emotional patterns of the financial environment. His ability to emotionally detach, look at the big picture objectively, and adjust his strategy rather than acting on impulse was what allowed him to become one of the most successful traders in history.

This example from Kovner illustrates perfectly how to apply the concept of "taking a step back" in the face of seemingly impossible problems. Instead of allowing fear to take over, he was able to stop, relax, and assess the situation from an outside perspective, which allowed him to find a logical and profitable solution. This lesson is not only applicable to trading, but to any situation where pendulums try to pull us into impulsive or fear-based decisions.

Another practical tip is to use your imagination and a sense of humor to relieve the tension that these problems create. Imagine that the financial environment is like a sea full of penguins wandering around aimlessly, and you are another penguin, sailing among them. This image may seem absurd, but that is precisely why it helps break the seriousness of the problem and see it from a less stressful perspective. Sometimes, releasing the tension is all you need to find a solution.

Finally, remember that the real problem is not the obstacle itself, but how we perceive it. Most of the time, pendulums want us to think that we are trapped, that there is no easy solution and that we must continue to go around in circles. But you can look beyond, to see the doors that have always been there and to distance yourself from the situation, acting from a place of calm and clarity.

In the end, being a successful trader is not just about winning trades, but about knowing how to deal with problems without letting them consume you. It is not a matter of fighting harder, but of learning to look with different eyes and find the easiest way out when everything seems to get complicated. That is "taking distance", that is freeing yourself from the pendulum, and that is the key to finding easy solutions to problems that seemed impossible.

The Suspended State

When you manage to free yourself from the influence of destructive emotional patterns, you experience a sense of relief and newfound freedom. You are free from fear, greed, social pressure, and you finally seem to be able to operate without those emotional burdens that once haunted you. On the other hand, this new state can bring with it a surprise: you find yourself in a kind of vacuum, as if you were suspended in the air.

This happens because once you stop feeding the pendulums with your energy and going in the direction they were imposing on you, you lose the drive to constantly fight. You no longer feel swept along by the emotional currents of the financial environment, but at the same time, you may notice that you no longer have a clear goal or direction to move towards. The stress and anxiety that once dominated your life as a trader begins to fade, but you also realize that you are no longer at the center of the action, you don't feel as involved in what is happening around you.

It's an interesting state because even though you've gained freedom, you can also feel a little disconnected. Imagine that you were previously running on a hamster wheel, always struggling to keep up, but now you find yourself outside that wheel, free to walk wherever you want. The problem is that once you're off the wheel, it can feel like you don't have a specific destination to head towards.

This is something that many traders experience when they manage to detach themselves from the emotions of the financial system. The external pressure diminishes, but it is not always replaced by new goals or a clearer purpose. It is like when great investors reach a certain level of success and stability: they have stopped worrying about the fluctuations of the sector or the emotions of others, but sometimes they find themselves with a feeling of "What now?" They no longer have the worries they used to have, but they also no longer have the immediate motivation that drove them to continue trading.

Legendary trader Ed Seykota achieved tremendous financial and emotional independence in his career. After achieving great success, there came a time when he stepped away from active trading to pursue other passions, such as music and philosophy. However, Seykota always maintained the awareness that, although he had stepped away from the pendulums of the financial sphere, he could not simply stay in that void. He found new ways to motivate himself, to learn and to continue growing, now from a place of greater detachment and freedom.

This is where the importance of setting your own pendulums comes into play, those that truly benefit you and are aligned with your goals and values. You cannot completely escape these energies because they are part of the very structure of the financial system and life. But you can choose which ones to follow and how to interact with them consciously. Your freedom does not lie in being completely free of pendulums, but in knowing how to identify which ones are useful to you and which ones are not.

Instead of being swept along by the pendulums of fear, greed, or societal pressure, you can create your own goals and strategically align yourself with them. It's about actively choosing the lifelines that bring you closer to the success and happiness you seek as a trader, rather than continuing to run after the goals others impose on you. It's a shift in focus, but one that allows you to operate from a space of balance and clarity.

Imagine you are the captain of a ship. For a long time, you were sailing in turbulent waters, fighting against currents that constantly steered you off course. Now that you have freed yourself from those currents, you find yourself in a calm sea, with total freedom to decide where to go. The trick is not to stay still, not to stay suspended. You need to set a new course, one that is aligned with what you really want to achieve as an investor.

When I discovered this and found that absolute silence in my mind, when the frenzy to trade faded away, I realized the big lie that many "smoke sellers" try to sell us. That illusion that you can make a living from trading by trading just one or two hours a day, and then spend the rest of the time thinking about yachts, trips and luxury cars... that is pure marketing. The life of a real trader is not as they paint it to us.

If you don't have something else to motivate you, to push you to keep growing, trading will lose all meaning. The sand castle you built will crumble, and you'll start to question whether you really wanted to trade in the first place. Without clear goals, trading becomes a prison, an addiction to the emotions it generates.

This book was born precisely from that state, from that moment of total silence in which I asked myself: "Is this it?... And now what?". I realized that I needed something more, something that would motivate me to keep moving forward, so as not to get stuck in the void. Trading can be a path to growth, but only if you find a purpose beyond the simple act of trading. It is essential to have an internal engine that takes you further, that drives you to become a better version of yourself, both inside and outside the financial field.

The suspended state is not bad in itself, but if you are not aware of it, you can become stuck. To avoid this, you need to be proactive and set new goals, without letting the financial pendulums drag you back down. It is about operating from a place of autonomy, being true to your own path rather than following the flows of others.

The Art of Quantum Trading ∞ John Carballar

Summary

- Pendulums in trading are collective forces that influence traders' behavior by emotionally aligning them with a trend or current in the financial system.
- A pendulum feeds on the energy of investors, keeping them trapped in patterns of collective behavior, such as panic in a market crash or euphoria in a speculative bubble.
- Destructive pendulums in trading divert traders from their personal goals, pushing them to make decisions based on emotions, such as fear or greed, rather than objective analysis.
- Great investors, such as Warren Buffett and Bruce Kovner, have learned to operate independently of the financial pendulums, making decisions based on their own strategy, rather than following the crowd.
- To free yourself from destructive pendulums, you need to operate objectively, follow a clear plan, and be emotionally detached from the results.
- Financial pendulums can cause traders to get what they don't want. By reacting with fear or frustration to an adverse move, the trader tunes into the frequency of that pendulum and contributes to perpetuating the problem.
- The pendulum can swing or die when the trader acts unexpectedly, breaking the established script and changing his usual reaction to the situation.
- Problem-solving is easier when the trader stops immersing himself in the problem and looks at it with detachment. This allows him to see simple solutions that the pendulum of the problem was hiding.
- It is crucial to avoid falling into a suspended state once freedom from destructive pendulums has been achieved. This involves defining new objectives and continuing to move towards one's own goals, rather than remaining in inaction.
- The key to being a conscious trader is to recognize the influence of pendulums and act from a place of clarity and mental balance, avoiding being swept away by collective emotions.

Chapter III

The wave of fortune

There are times when everything seems to be going your way. The markets align in your favor, the moves are precisely what you expected, and the opportunities seem to multiply. Vadim calls this "the wave of fortune," and I want you to think of it as that positive streak that naturally comes along occasionally and can lead to a series of successes. The wave of fortune is a force that, unlike pendulums, is not interested in your energy or manipulating your emotions. It is like an ocean wave that comes to gently and effortlessly carry you to shore, if you choose to float with it. In trading, this happens when a set of favorable circumstances spontaneously presents itself and allows you to take advantage of the momentum without the feeling of fighting the market.

It's important to understand that, like pendulums, the wave of fortune has no vested interest in your success or failure. It's not going to sit there waiting for you, nor is it going to force you to follow it. The wave simply passes, and it's up to you to decide whether you want to ride it or let it go. Think of those times when a piece of positive news favors the stock or cryptocurrency you've already bought, and suddenly the price rises rapidly, allowing you to collect profits almost effortlessly. This is the wave of fortune in action.

An interesting case of this type of phenomenon is that of George Soros, known for his ability to anticipate macroeconomic movements. During the episode known as "Black Wednesday" in 1992, Soros recognized the weaknesses of the Bank of England and the overvaluation of the British pound. Instead of trying to predict every market move, Soros positioned himself in a way that he could take advantage of the opportunity if conditions aligned in his favor. When the devaluation finally happened, Soros was ready, he flowed with the event and made a massive profit. He did not try to manipulate the circumstances, but rather he went with the flow of fortune, and that ability to recognize the right moment was key to his success.

The key to benefiting from the waves of fortune is to learn to recognize these moments and not sabotage yourself. Often, when we have a good streak, the fear of losing or the feeling that it is "too good to be true" prevents us from taking full advantage of it. This situation translates into closing positions too soon due to uncertainty about a correction, or avoiding risks when the context seems favorable. It is essential that, when you find yourself in the middle of a wave of fortune, you trust the process and let yourself go, without trying to control every detail.

This doesn't mean acting recklessly. Going with the flow also means maintaining a sense of balance and keeping in mind that favorable conditions don't last forever. It's important to know when to take profits and how to protect yourself against potential changes. However, it's also essential to avoid excessive doubt or self-sabotage that leads us to walk away from opportunities simply because everything seems to be going too well.

Think of the wave of fortune as that favorable wind that blows through your sails when you're sailing. You can adjust your sails and make the most of it, or you can ignore it, worry about possible storms, and stay put. Recognizing and taking advantage of the wave of fortune can be the difference between a single successful trade and a series of events that take you to a new level of achievement.

Another interesting analogy is to think of the surfer who waits for the perfect wave. When he sees the wave coming, he prepares himself, gathers momentum, and confidently rides it, letting the energy of the wave carry him toward the shore. He doesn't fight the wave, nor does he try to control it; he simply aligns himself with it and rides it. When you find yourself on a positive streak, you should act like that surfer, ready to take advantage of the energy that carries you forward without resistance or fear.

The real skill lies in knowing how to keep yourself clear of the destructive pendulums that try to divert you, and being alert to those waves of good fortune that pass by from time to time. If you recognize them and allow yourself to ride them, you will be able to experience unexpected growth, and above all, without the emotional drain that constant battles against the market entail.

It's also important not to confuse the wave of fortune with fleeting luck. Luck can appear spontaneously, but the wave of fortune is an alignment of events that you can consciously identify and take advantage of. It requires you to be present and attentive to market signals, to trust your analysis, and not to let fear stop you. It's knowing that, although you can't control all the variables, you can maximize your chances by being in the right place at the right time, with the right attitude.

Antipode to the pendulum: There are no constructive pendulums

Now that we have explored the wave of fortune, it is important to understand what makes it different from pendulums. These energies are collective entities that feed off the energy of those who attach themselves to them. Most pendulums are destructive because they seek to control our actions and emotions to gain energy, regardless of whether they lead us to make decisions that are harmful to ourselves.

A valid question is: are there pendulums that are constructive? The answer is complex because a pendulum can only be considered constructive in relation to itself, but not necessarily to its adherents. This means that even though a structure may appear positive – such as a sports club or a learning community – it still requires the energy of its members to keep it active and moving.

For example, you might join a trading group that focuses on a certain strategy. As long as all members are aligned and continue to contribute their time and energy, the group thrives. But if at some point you decide that strategy is no longer right for you and you walk away from the group, the pendulum loses some of its force. That is, the collective force is maintained as long as it receives energy, but it is not necessarily designed to benefit its members individually, but to perpetuate itself.

The wave of fortune, on the other hand, does not require your energy to exist. It does not ask for anything in return, it simply presents itself, and you decide whether you want to take advantage of it or not. This makes the wave of fortune a different and more beneficial phenomenon for the individual, since there is no dependency relationship or hidden interest. While pendulums drag you into their dynamics, the wave of fortune propels you without demands, allowing you to navigate towards a more favorable state in your life and in your trading.

Understanding this difference is crucial, as it allows us to know when we are being pulled by an external force and when we are actually taking advantage of an opportunity that is presented to us without strings attached. The key is to recognize these patterns, avoid getting caught in the games of the pendulums, and learn to flow with the waves of good fortune when they present themselves. It is an exercise in awareness and choice, which can make the difference between operating under constant pressure or enjoying the opportunities that the market has to offer naturally.

In short, the wave of fortune in trading is that series of favorable circumstances that allows us to move forward without the emotional burden and wear and tear that pendulums usually bring. It is about taking advantage of those moments, being alert to opportunities, and allowing ourselves to flow with the market without unnecessary resistance. The ability to identify and navigate these waves of good fortune can be a powerful tool for any trader seeking not only financial results, but also a more harmonious and rewarding trading experience.

The Boomerang: What you think comes back to you in trading

In the world of trading, our emotions and thoughts play a much more powerful role than we might imagine. Many times, without realizing it, we feed situations that we want to avoid simply because we are so focused on them that they become the center of our energy emission. Like a boomerang, those negative thoughts and feelings come back to us again and again, leading us into a spiral of bad decisions and unfortunate results.

It's natural that when we're trading in the financial world, worries, fears, or even frustrations arise. We've all been there: the fear of missing a trade, the anxiety of seeing a trend go against us, or the constant worry about volatility. These thoughts become destructive pendulums that not only affect our mental state, but also bind us to outcomes that, ironically, are the very ones we wanted to avoid. This is the boomerang effect: whatever we focus our attention and energy on comes back to us, for better or worse.

Imagine you're having a losing streak, and you're constantly thinking about how to avoid further losses. You tell yourself, "I don't want to keep losing money. I'm sick of every trade going wrong." Even though it may seem like your focus is on avoiding the problem, you're actually giving it energy and attracting more of the same. By focusing so much on what you don't want, you align yourself with that frequency and end up in situations that reflect those same fears: more losses, more frustration, more anxiety.

A clear example could be when a trader decides not to lose any more money and starts avoiding any trade that involves minimal risk. He focuses so much on avoiding losses that he loses sight of opportunities that could lead to profits. This fear and risk-averse mindset keeps him trapped, unable to act when a good opportunity presents itself, and thus, ironically, he ends up losing more than he would have lost if he had acted with a balanced and conscious mindset.

The key is to change your focus. Instead of thinking about what you want to avoid, start thinking about what you would like to achieve. For example, if your goal is to have successful trades, focus on how you could improve your strategy, how you could learn from experiences, and what aspects of your trading plan you can strengthen. Visualize your successful trades, think about the steps that will lead you to those results, and be grateful for every opportunity you are presented with to improve. This positive mindset will change the frequency of your energy emission and attract better results, just like the boomerang, but this time with a positive charge.

This also applies to other aspects of everyday life. Let's say you live in a place you don't like, and you constantly complain about how bad it is.

—Ugh, the neighbors already have me angry with their noise every day, the bathroom is blocked and, to top it off, there are problems with the electricity service.

Chances are, even if you move, you'll still find fault with your new home because you carry with you the same negative energy and focus on what's wrong. If you only focus on the difficulties and risks, no matter how many new strategies you try or how much capital you raise, there will always be something keeping you stuck in an unsatisfying reality.

The right mindset is not to ignore problems or act as if everything is perfect, but to learn to direct your thoughts in a way that allows you to align yourself with what you really want. Instead of fighting the financial environment or feeling frustrated because things don't go the way you expected, accept the circumstances as they are, learn from them, and focus on the opportunities you can take advantage of. A conscious trader is not one who avoids risk at all costs, but one who understands when and how to act without being carried away by emotional pendulums.

You could think of this like tuning into a radio station. If you constantly tune into the frequency of fear and frustration, that's what you'll hear and what you'll attract into your life. But if you change the frequency and start broadcasting positive, success-focused thoughts, your reality will begin to reflect that change. In trading, the frequency you choose to tune into determines the kind of results you get. Every thought is like a broadcast that eventually comes back to you, so make sure that what you send out into the universe is what you want to receive.

To go even deeper, consider the example of Bruce Kovner, one of the most successful traders in history. Early in his career, Kovner experienced losses that nearly put him out of business. But instead of worrying about losing more, he decided to think of each loss as a lesson. He learned to manage risk and better understand the movements of the financial system. Kovner didn't get stuck in the frequency of frustration or fear; instead, he focused on improving his strategy and adjusting his mental approach toward success. This allowed him to not only recover, but eventually become one of the most recognized traders in the world. The attitude of constant learning and the ability to see beyond mistakes was what led him to align himself with a positive frequency and, consequently, to achieve extraordinary results.

Another important aspect to consider is the power of gratitude. We often underestimate how powerful it can be to simply be thankful for what we have and what we've learned. Even if you're not where you want to be, being thankful for the lessons you've learned and the opportunities presented to you can help you shift your focus. Gratitude shifts your emission frequency, moving you away from the pendulum of discontent and toward an abundance mindset. When you are thankful for every trade, whether it's a winner or a loser, you're telling the universe that you value the process and are ready to receive more of the good stuff.

Gratitude also has a direct impact on how you perceive risk and opportunity. Instead of seeing risk as a threat, you begin to see it as an essential part of the growth process. The most successful traders are not those who avoid risk, but those who know how to manage it and see it as an opportunity for growth. This attitude is what allows you to tune into a higher frequency, where the wave of fortune has a better chance of taking you towards your goals.

Finally, becoming aware of your thoughts and how they impact your results isn't something that happens overnight. It requires consistent practice and a willingness to change ingrained thought patterns. Whenever you find yourself falling into the trap of negative thoughts, stop and redirect your focus. Visualize what you want to achieve, rather than what you fear. Do this over and over again, until it becomes a habit. Over time, you'll see your thoughts boomerang back with positive results because you'll have changed the quality of energy you're sending out into the world.

In conclusion, the boomerang concept reminds us that everything we put out, whether it be positive or negative energy, will come back to us eventually. If you want your trading experience to be fulfilling and productive, start by controlling your mind, aligning your thoughts with what you want to achieve, not what you fear. By doing so, you will stop feeding destructive pendulums and start creating an environment conducive to your own success. A positive mindset is the key to attracting the right opportunities and growing on this challenging path.

What you think and feel has a profound impact on the results you achieve. Your mental state, whether positive or negative, is reflected in the way you trade and, consequently, in the decisions you make in the trading arena. Throughout the day, it is effortless to fall into a routine of focusing on what goes wrong: a trade that did not go as you expected, a trend that suddenly changed, or the constant bombardment of news affecting the markets. But instead of being carried away by these "destructive pendulums," it is crucial to develop the ability to tune into what can be positive and beneficial for you.

Let's go back to the example where your mind is like a radio receiver. If you tune your frequency to thoughts of frustration, fear or worry, those will be the "programs" you will listen to all day long. The financial world, like life itself, has it all: moments of calm, unexpected storms, brilliant opportunities and also disguised deceptions. The key to being a successful trader is learning to tune into the frequency of opportunity and not that of the pendulum of fear or greed.

Imagine you are walking through a forest full of flowers and also poisonous brambles. You can choose what to pick: the brambles, which represent negative emotions, or the flowers, which symbolize the opportunities and joy of each moment. If you constantly focus on what is wrong, like those brambles, you will carry thorns that hurt you and make your path difficult. But if you decide to pick the flowers, you will see how your energy changes, and you begin to attract positive things into your life. In trading, picking "flowers" means focusing on what the environment offers you: the opportunities to learn, to grow, and to take advantage of favorable movements.

Let's look at a concrete example. Let's say you're on a losing streak and every trade seems to go against you. It's easy to fall into the trap of starting to think:

— "The market is against me, I can't win, I always lose, maybe it's a scam and my broker is making me lose on purpose."

These thoughts not only feed a negative pendulum, but they also keep you tied to a frequency that will only attract more losses and frustration. However, if you decide to change your approach and see each failed trade as a lesson, as a necessary step to improve your strategy, then you are picking flowers instead of thorns. You are tuning your frequency to the wave of fortune, creating a state of mind where opportunities begin to appear.

Another way to keep your stream positive is to be careful about how you react to the information you receive. Bad news and sensational information tend to grab our attention because they play on our survival instinct, generating fear or euphoria. These emotional impulses can be extremely dangerous. Instead of reacting to every headline or market fluctuation, try to maintain an observer's stance.

Take in the information without letting it control your emotions. Instead, when you find a piece of good news, an opportunity, or even a small breakthrough, put your attention on it. Analyze it, give it only the necessary importance, and let that positive energy guide your decisions.

Just like a surfer waiting for the perfect wave, in trading you need to have the patience and clarity to recognize the waves of fortune when they appear. If you are constantly worried about small waves that throw you unbalanced, you will never be able to surf the big wave that will take you to the shore of success. To be prepared, you must maintain a positive state of mind and an attitude of expectation towards the good. This does not mean ignoring the risks, but learning to see beyond them and recognize the opportunities.

The right mindset also involves being prepared for challenges. Imagine a ship captain sailing through turbulent waters. If the captain focuses only on the danger of the waves, he will miss the opportunity to steer his ship into calmer waters. Similarly, as a trader, you need to stay calm and focused on your goals, even when market conditions are adverse. Every storm will eventually pass, and if you stay on the right track, you will find the opportunity to sail into more favorable waters.

Being a transmitter of positive energy is not only about receiving the good, but also about projecting it. An investor who maintains a positive attitude and a calm approach transmits that energy to the environment and to those around him. Imagine that every thought and every emotion you have is like a seed that you plant in your environment.

If you cultivate seeds of uncertainty, fear or frustration, you will generate more circumstances that feed these emotions. But if you plant seeds of confidence, patience and optimism, you will see how opportunities that reflect that energy begin to blossom.

It is also important to understand that the trading world is full of ups and downs, and what determines your success is not avoiding the downs, but how you choose to deal with them. Think of the great traders who, in the midst of downtrends, stood firm and took advantage of the downturns to build solid positions.

Warren Buffett has always emphasized the importance of being "greedy when others are afraid." This philosophy is based on not being influenced by collective panic, but on identifying opportunities where others only see danger. This is a way to tune in to the wave of fortune, even when the general environment seems negative.

Remember also the importance of consistency. It is not enough to transmit positive energy once; you need to do it every day. Maintain the right attitude every morning before you begin your trading day. Some successful traders use rituals such as meditation, visualization of goals, or simply going over a clear plan of action before opening their platforms. These practices help keep the mind in the right state and avoid falling into the traps of destructive pendulums that may arise during the day.

In conclusion, to be successful, it is essential to learn to control our emission of mental energy. By focusing on the positive, on the opportunities, and learning to let go of the negative, you will be creating a frequency that will attract success. Remember that trading is no different from the rest of life: what you put your attention and energy on is what ends up growing. Tune into the right frequency and let the wave of fortune carry you towards your goals. Mental discipline and a positive approach are powerful tools that, when used well, will allow you to navigate even the roughest seas and find the success you seek.

Preparation rituals: Aligning yourself with the Wave of Success in Trading

In the world of trading, as in many other areas of life, the way we prepare and the beliefs we nurture can have a huge impact on our performance. Sometimes, the small rituals we adopt, without realizing it, function as a kind of "tuner" that helps us connect with a positive frequency and align ourselves with the wave of luck. These symbolic acts, even if they do not have a direct impact on the financial environment, can change our mindset and help us flow better with the surrounding circumstances.

Let's think, for example, about salespeople who have certain "rituals" at the start of their day, such as giving a discount to the first customer to attract more sales. Basically, what they are looking for is to align themselves with a positive frequency from the beginning of the day. If they manage to make a successful first sale, this gives them confidence and allows them to enter a kind of streak of good fortune. These types of rituals have no magic in themselves, but they allow the person to adjust their mindset towards success.

In trading, this also applies. Experienced traders often develop daily routines that help them feel aligned with a winning mindset. It can be something as simple as making a coffee while reviewing their charts, doing breathing exercises before they start trading, or even writing affirmations about their goals for the day. These rituals don't directly affect market dynamics, but they do have a huge impact on how a trader feels and behaves during trading.

Let's think of a specific example. Stanley Druckenmiller, known for his ability to read macroeconomic trends, always shares the importance of preparing psychologically before each session. Although he doesn't mention it as a "magic ritual," his approach of reviewing all the details and entering a confident state of mind could be considered a way of tuning into the frequency of success. If we start the day with mental clarity, we have already taken a big step towards riding the wave of fortune.

Another practice that many traders use is positive affirmations. Before starting their day, they tell themselves phrases like "I am calm and clear about trading," "I trust my strategy and my decisions," or "I am aligned with the opportunities of the day." Just like salespeople who brush their products with money believing in a successful sale, these affirmations help program our minds to act from a state of confidence and agreeing with opportunities. It's not magic, it's simple psychology: when you believe in what you do, you transmit that confidence, and both you and those around you perceive that emission.

The key is to understand that these rituals work because they allow the trader to focus on the process and not the outcome. By creating a routine that tunes your mind to the frequency of a "wave of success," you can trade with less stress and more clarity. This makes you less vulnerable to destructive pendulums, which tend to appear when we are insecure or frustrated.

Another good analogy is that of an athlete warming up before an important match. Warming up doesn't guarantee victory, but it helps the body and mind get into the best possible condition to face the challenge. Our daily rituals serve a similar function. Proper preparation allows us to enter trading from a position of balance, ready to seize opportunities when the wave of fortune passes in front of us.

Also, let's think about Formula 1 drivers before a race. They have a number of rituals and preparations, from checking every detail of the car to visualizing the circuit layout. These rituals help them get into an optimal state of mind, focused and ready to act quickly. In trading, having a preparation routine before trading begins or before executing a transaction serves the same purpose: it allows us to focus, reduce distractions, and trade with confidence.

We can also mention the example of ancient sailors who prepared themselves meticulously before setting sail into the unknown. They performed rituals, not because they thought magic would control the wind, but because preparation and concentration helped them face any challenge they encountered on the high seas. For us, like them, every day is a journey into the unknown, and our rituals function as that preparation that gives us peace of mind and allows us to feel ready for any eventuality.

Rituals also serve an important emotional function. In an environment like trading, where emotions can be our worst enemy, having a routine helps keep us calm. Rituals give us a sense of control in an environment that is, in many ways, unpredictable. Knowing that you have done your homework, reviewed all the details, and entered into trades with the right mindset can be the difference between a successful trade and one filled with impulsive mistakes.

In short, it's not about blindly trusting a "magic ritual" or a superstition. Rather, it's about using small actions that help us mentally tune into the energy of success. These rituals allow us to flow with the dynamics of the market instead of fighting them, to seize opportunities instead of letting them pass us by, and to stay away from the destructive pendulums that seek to divert us from our goals. It's a matter of preparing, generating a positive mindset, and allowing yourself to ride that wave of good fortune when it presents itself.

The next time you face a trading session, reflect on what your rituals are. What do you do to get into the right frame of mind? It can be something as simple as taking a few minutes to breathe deeply, reviewing your trading plan, or visualizing a successful day. Whatever it is, make sure it helps you tune into that frequency of success because how you start your day can make all the difference in how you end it. When you manage to align yourself with the wave of fortune, you not only trade with more confidence, but you also allow yourself to enjoy the process, and that, at the end of the day, is what really matters.

The Art of Quantum Trading ∞ John Carballar

Summary

- The wave of fortune is an accumulation of favorable circumstances in the "variation space" of trading. It is presented as a series of positive events that can boost our success in trading.

- The cascade of opportunities continues only if the first success generates confidence and enthusiasm in the trader, tuning him to the frequency of success.

- Destructive pendulums try to push you away from the wave of fortune, filling your mind with doubts and negative emotions.

- The detachment of pendulums gives you the freedom to make conscious decisions and align yourself with the wave of good fortune, maximizing your chances of success.

- By accepting and transmitting negative energy, you keep yourself trapped in unfavorable lifelines; by transmitting positive energy, you create an environment that favors your trading goals. Your thoughts always come back to you like a boomerang: what you send out into the world of investments, comes back.

- Consistency in remembering your goals and tuning into positive energy is the key to staying on top of the wave. Systematic practice and creating rituals or routines help reinforce this habit and keep you aligned successfully in every operation.

Chapter IV

Keep the balance

In trading, as in life, you are often your own worst enemy. We often create unnecessary problems and obstacles for ourselves and then wear ourselves out trying to overcome them. But what if, instead of focusing on those problems we create ourselves, we learned not to create them in the first place? What if, instead of constantly struggling, we focused on maintaining balance?

In nature, everything tends towards balance. If there is a difference in atmospheric pressure, wind is generated to level it out. If there is a difference in temperature, heat moves to balance out. This law of stability is universal and affects both the physical and mental world. In life, as in trading, if "excessive potential" is generated, the forces of the universe act to restore balance. And those forces can be relentless.

"Excessive potentials," as we already know, are created when we give too much importance to something. This happens when we attribute exaggerated qualities, both positive and negative, to an event or outcome.

This happens when we give a disproportionate value to a specific trade. Let's say you decide that a particular entry is crucial to proving your worth as a trader. Automatically, you have created excessive potential. You have put too much weight on that trade, and this destabilizes the balance.

The more importance you give to a trade, the more internal tension you generate. This tension creates a resistance that affects your mental clarity and decision-making ability. In trading, this translates into irrational behaviors: moving the stop loss out of fear of losing, taking profits early out of anxiety, or overtrading to recover a loss. The environment perceives this destabilization and acts like the balancing forces in nature, leading the result towards an outcome that is usually not favorable.

To avoid falling into this trap, it is important to view each trade as a small part of a larger process, not as the only opportunity for success. Traders who manage to be consistent over time do so not by having one exceptional winning trade, but by maintaining a strategy that is repeated with discipline and balance. This approach lessens the emotional burden and allows each trade to be executed from a calmer state of mind.

Furthermore, it is crucial to understand that each trade is just one statistic in a larger set. Successful traders have a mindset that is oriented toward probability and statistics, not the emotion of a single trade. By reducing the importance placed on each individual trade, excessive potential is reduced and rational, well-informed decision-making is made easier.

Mental balance is also broken when we try to control too much. It is important to remember that we cannot predict or control market conditions; the only thing we can control is our reaction to them. Imagine that you are standing on the edge of a cliff. If you start to feel too afraid, you generate excessive potential: a part of you wants to move away from the edge, while another part feels an inexplicable force dragging you down.

This is the effect of the forces of balance trying to eliminate that tension. Something similar happens when you attempt to force an outcome in your trading: by attempting to control every move, you only generate more tension and fear, and the environment itself, in its own way, "pushes" you towards an outcome that you probably do not want.

Rather than trying to control every trade or outcome, a much more effective alternative is to act from a state of emotional harmony, taking each step with confidence but not desperation. This means setting your strategies, defining your entry and exit levels, and then allowing the process to take its course. This is what I call "letting go." It's not about being indifferent or acting carelessly, but about not allowing one trade to consume all of your mental and emotional energy.

This approach of letting go of control also has a positive impact on risk management. Traders who seek to control every aspect of their trading often make the mistake of constantly adjusting their positions, moving their stoploss or changing their targets, which can increase risk and losses. While there are strategies where it is valid to move the stop loss to protect an already profitable position, it should never be extended beyond what was initially planned. Instead, letting go of the need to control every detail allows you to trade in a more structured way and trust your prior analysis.

It is essential to understand that acting from a balanced perspective does not mean being mediocre or working without effort, but rather being impeccable in what you do, without generating unnecessary tension. Impeccability means complying with your rules and processes, doing your analysis with rigor and executing with discipline. But it also means knowing how to rest, knowing how to disconnect when there are no clear opportunities, and not overoperating.

Let's think of an investor who trades without unnecessary attachments. This trader sticks to his plan and follows his strategy in a disciplined manner, but he doesn't place an unreasonable value on each trade. On the contrary, he acts from a position of confidence in himself and his method, without falling into the trap of letting each trade defines his worth as a trader. This approach reduces pressure, minimizes the risk of impulsive mistakes, and allows the trader to stay aligned with his "wave of fortune."

Impeccability also means being present in every moment of the operation without the burden of unreasonable expectations. When you act with impeccability, you are not chasing perfection, but rather doing the best you can with the information and tools you have. This mindset not only improves your performance, but also reduces the emotional drain that comes with trying to reach an unattainable level of perfection.

Being impeccable also means being honest with yourself about your limits. It's important to know when it's time to pause and when it's time to act. Sometimes, the best decision you can make as an investor is to do nothing. This is part of impeccability: recognizing that the market doesn't always present clear opportunities, and that in those moments, inaction is the best course of action.

It is common to see some traders working themselves to exhaustion, trading without rest, completely immersing themselves in their activity, and yet the results are not forthcoming. This lack of results is often a reflection of the excessive potentials created by the excessive importance they attribute to their performance. In nature, rigidity is synonymous with fragility, while flexibility allows for adaptation and survival. Similarly, in trading, those who are too hard on themselves and do not allow for some flexibility end up generating a resistance that prevents them from moving forward.

The solution lies in focusing on the process, rather than the outcome. If you manage to be impeccable in executing your strategy, following your rules, and properly managing your risk, then you are doing your part. The rest depends on factors you cannot control. This mindset allows you to operate from a state of emotional harmony, where there are no more excessive potentials destabilizing your energy.

Flow in trading also means accepting that there will be times of uncertainty and that you won't always be right. Accepting the fact that conditions are unpredictable allows you to let go of the need to always be right and instead focus on how to manage what the environment throws at you. This mental flexibility is what separates traders who survive and thrive from those who burn out quickly.

Learning to flow also involves adapting to different situations that arise. Not every day is a good day to trade; there are times of high volatility and others of consolidation, and it is important to know when to take advantage of an opportunity and when to stay on the sidelines. This ability to adapt is key to staying in the game for the long term.

It is crucial to remember that trading is just one part of your life, not your whole life. Giving it too much importance can cause other relevant areas, such as health, relationships, and personal well-being, to be negatively affected. A balanced trader knows when to step away from trading, when to take a break, and when to focus on other activities that energize and make them happy. This perspective allows them to maintain a healthier state of mind, which translates into better decision-making when they return to trading.

Another important point is to avoid comparing yourself to other traders. Everyone has their own path, and what works for one won't necessarily work for another. Constant comparison is another source of over-potential that creates tension and frustration. Instead of focusing on what others are doing, focus on your own progress and how you can improve your skills and processes. Keep an eye on your own evolution and learn to value your achievements, no matter how small.

A healthy outlook also means understanding that losses are an inevitable part of the process. The best traders in the world lose money on some trades, but they don't let those losses define their career. They view losses as learning opportunities, evaluate what went wrong, and adjust their strategies to avoid making the same mistakes in the future.

Discontent and self-criticism

Self-dissatisfaction is a common trap that many traders fall into. This manifests itself as dissatisfaction with one's own achievements or qualities and a constant struggle against personal imperfections. We all have flaws, and it's natural to be aware of them, but when flaws become the focus of our attention, they end up generating "excessive potential." This concept implies that we devote so much energy to our shortcomings that, inevitably, the mental balance is disrupted, and the result is often the opposite of what we desire. The more we fight against our own imperfections, the more we increase that potential, and the forces that try to balance it often do so in ways that do not always favor us.

Think of a trader who is constantly frustrated because he can't help but feel fear during a trade. That fear becomes his enemy, and he tries to suppress it, hide it, or fight it. The result is that he becomes more anxious, his decisions become worse, and his trading is affected by this constant attempt to hide his vulnerability. It's like when someone sets out to hide that he's nervous during a public presentation: the more he fights the nervousness, the more obvious it becomes and the harder it becomes to control. It's a vicious cycle where the internal struggle only intensifies the problem, affecting not only the ability to concentrate but also overall performance.

The Art of Quantum Trading ∞ John Carballar

This phenomenon is not unique to trading; anyone who tries to fight their emotions knows how exhausting this process can be.

The key here is not to ignore our imperfections, but to embrace them. If we recognize that fear is part of the process and observe it without judgment, that fear loses its power. The energy that was previously spent fighting is freed up, and we can focus it on improving other aspects of our trading, such as our technical analysis or risk management. It's like a gardener who decides to stop fighting weeds and instead focuses on nurturing and strengthening healthy plants; in doing so, the weeds lose prominence and the garden becomes more vigorous.

Imagine that, instead of constantly focusing on the mistakes you make during your analysis, you decide to spend more time reinforcing your effective strategies. Little by little, the mistakes lose relevance and your trading becomes stronger. This doesn't mean that the mistakes will disappear, but that the energy you previously spent beating yourself up becomes a tool for learning and improving.

In everyday life, we can also see examples of how accepting our imperfections frees us from the weight of internal struggle. Think of a person who feels uncomfortable with their physical appearance. Every time they try to hide or fight those feelings, they feel more tense and insecure. On the other hand, when they accept their imperfections and focus on what they can improve, such as their health and general well-being, they begin to feel more at peace with themselves.

That acceptance transforms the energy they previously spent on self-criticism into a source of motivation to do positive things. Similarly, a trader who focuses on what they can control, such as their preparation and discipline, and accepts what they cannot, such as the volatility of the environment, will be better positioned both mentally and emotionally to trade.

When we are dissatisfied with our achievements, but to an extent that drives us to improve without punishing ourselves, the balance is maintained. This mild dissatisfaction is the fuel for self-perfection. However, when dissatisfaction turns into constant self-reproach and self-criticism, a conflict arises between our mind and our essence. The soul, which is our purest and freest part, does not understand judgment; it simply is. The mind, on the other hand, often imposes expectations and demands on us that, when not met, translate into merciless criticism of ourselves. This internal conflict can be devastating for a trader, leading to a state of emotional and mental blockage. It is important to recognize that excessive self-criticism only leads to paralysis and exhaustion, and does not contribute positively to personal growth.

To avoid this situation, it is essential to forgive ourselves for our imperfections. If you cannot yet, love yourself as you are, at least stop fighting against yourself. Accepting yourself is the first step to getting your essence and your mind to work together, instead of being in constant opposition. In the context of trading, this means allowing yourself to make mistakes without punishing yourself for them.

Think of a child learning to walk: every time they fall, they get up and try again, without berating themselves for having stumbled. In the same way, as traders, we must learn to get up from every mistake, taking the lesson without the weight of guilt. Every mistake can be seen as a step forward if it is approached with a constructive mindset, learning from each fall and applying that learning to improve next time. This is the difference between traders who eventually achieve success and those who are stuck in a cycle of frustration: the ability to learn and adapt without getting caught up in self-judgment.

Someone might say, "Okay, I'll stop fighting my imperfections, but how do I develop my virtues? I can't stop growing as a person." The answer is simple: keep working on your positive qualities without focusing on destroying your flaws.

When you stop spending energy fighting yourself, all that energy is channeled into developing your capabilities. Instead of obsessing about not being brave enough, for example, focus on developing a better trading strategy that will give you the confidence you seek. It's as if, instead of trying to remove the darkness from a room, you simply turned on a light. This analogy is fundamental: darkness is not fought directly, but illuminated. Focusing on virtues and the positive allows less developed areas to lose weight.

This approach seems trivial, but many traders waste an enormous amount of energy fighting against themselves, trying to hide their insecurities, or forcing themselves to be someone they are not. They condemn themselves to carrying a heavy load, as if they were titans holding up the sky. But when they allow themselves to be who they are, that load lightens and life—and trading—becomes much simpler. Energy that was once devoted to internal struggle is redirected to skill development and continuous improvement. Imagine constantly trying to swim against the current: the effort exhausts you, and you barely make any progress.

However, if you learn to move with the current, using its force to your advantage, the ride becomes much smoother and less draining. This does not mean that you should passively accept everything that happens; rather, it is about recognizing when it is wiser to go with the flow and when it is necessary to act decisively.

An important aspect of discontent is how it affects our relationship with the outside world. If we are dissatisfied with ourselves, we create internal conflict; but if we are dissatisfied with the world, we enter into conflict with the "pendulums," those external forces that feed off our negative energy. Just like in trading, if we continually complain about environmental conditions or how unfair price movements are, we enter a negative spiral that leads us to operate from a place of frustration and anger.

This makes us vulnerable and keeps us away from the best opportunities, as our decisions are conditioned by destructive emotions. Complaints about conditions are often a way of giving power to external circumstances, which is extremely counterproductive. When we allow the environment to have complete control over our emotions, we lose our ability to consciously respond and take action. Imagine you are a sailor facing a storm: if you focus only on how unfair and violent the storm is, you will miss the opportunity to maneuver your ship to safety. Embracing the storm, preparing, and adjusting your sails will give you a better chance of survival.

On the contrary, if we learn to rejoice in the little things, even in difficult times, we emit a constructive energy that leads us to better paths in life. It is like a trader who, instead of cursing a loss, accepts it and focuses on what he has learned from that experience.

That positive attitude not only improves his emotional state, but also puts him in a better position to take advantage of future opportunities. The key is to replace the habit of criticizing with the habit of appreciating. When you find yourself in a difficult situation, look for something good, no matter how small. Make it a game, and over time, the habit of finding the positive will replace that of focusing on the negative. A good example of this is keeping a gratitude journal, where at the end of each day you write down three positive things that happened during the day, even if they are small. This practice gradually changes your perspective to a more positive and constructive one.

Furthermore, this technique not only improves the emotional state, but also has a direct impact on the quality of our trading decisions, as it allows us to keep our mind clear and focused on what really matters.

Another point to keep in mind is that a positive attitude doesn't mean ignoring problems or living in a bubble of unrealistic optimism. Rather, it's about changing the way we react to difficulties. Instead of getting stuck in negative thinking, we learn to accept reality as it is and find a way forward. It's like driving on a bumpy road: you can complain about every bump, stop and blame the road, or you can simply adjust your speed and direction to get to your destination in the best possible way. This flexibility and adaptability are critical in both trading and everyday life. As traders, we must be prepared to face moments of high volatility or unexpected events without losing our composure. Instead of fighting the inevitable, we must learn to adapt quickly and take advantage of what the environment has to offer.

Finally, remember that we are all guests in this world. No one has the right to judge what they have not created, and this includes judging ourselves harshly. In trading, as in life, it is not about being a submissive sheep, but neither is it about meeting everything with hostility. If conditions seem to be against you, do not fight them; rather, learn to move with them, accept their twists and turns, and adapt. Like King Solomon, who wore a ring with the inscription "And this too shall pass," remember that every situation, good or bad, is temporary. Stay calm, accept the present moment, and keep moving forward. This acceptance is not resignation, but a smart way to approach challenges without wasting valuable energy on fruitless struggles.

As traders, our ability to adapt and keep moving, no matter the circumstances, is what really makes the difference eventually. It is important to understand that flexibility is not synonymous with weakness; It is a strength that allows us to face difficult situations with a clear mind and a calm heart, and better positions us to take advantage of opportunities when they arise.

Emotional Dependencies in Trading

An idealization of the world is the flip side of discontent. Sometimes, traders fall into the trap of seeing everything in a rosy light, and many things seem better than they really are. In these cases, "excessive potential" is generated because we are overestimating a situation or creating unrealistic expectations. Idealizing means overestimating, placing something on a pedestal, worshiping or even creating an idol. This idealization, although seemingly harmless, creates a relationship of dependency that can become harmful, especially in the trading field.

The love that generates and directs the world differs from idealization in that, paradoxically, it is impassive. Absolute love is a feeling without the right of possession, an admiration without adoration. In other words, it does not generate relationships of dependence between the one who loves and the object of his love. This simple formula can help you determine where genuine feeling ends and idealization begins.

Imagine you are walking through a valley surrounded by mountains, covered in greenery and full of flowers. You admire the scenery, breathe in the fresh air, and your soul is filled with happiness and tranquility. That is love. However, if you start to pluck the flowers, collect them to make perfumes, or even to sell them, you create a dependency. The flowers are no longer simply part of the landscape, but an object that you want to possess or use. At that point, pure love turns into idealization and dependency. That love you felt when you were simply looking at the valley disappears. Do you feel the difference?

This same concept applies to trading. It's natural to feel excited or motivated by an asset that looks promising, but when that excitement turns into a need for that asset to live up to our expectations, we fall into the trap of dependency. Many traders idealize certain instruments, believing they will always go up, or they blindly trust a strategy, expecting it to work, no matter what the conditions are. This creates "excess potential," an energy that will eventually be balanced by market forces, and the result is often disappointment or loss.

Idealization creates expectations that are not always met. When we idealize a trade, an asset, or even our ability as traders, we are creating an emotional dependence. If the result is not what we expected, the emotional blow is much stronger because we have not only lost money, but we have also seen our expectations crumble. On the other hand, the love for the process, for learning and improving every day, allows us to enjoy trading without depending on a specific result.

Think about how this difference is reflected in everyday life. Imagine a relationship where one of the partners idealizes the other, believing that they will always be there, that they will always make them happy and that they will never have any flaws. This idealization creates an emotional dependence that, when faced with reality (where we are all human and have flaws), generates conflict and disappointment. In a healthy relationship, on the other hand, one loves the other person as they are, without idealizing them, accepting their virtues and their flaws. This impassive love, without unrealistic expectations, is what allows the relationship to be authentic and lasting.

Similarly, as traders, we must learn to love the process of trading without idealizing outcomes. We must accept that there will be losses and that conditions will not always move in our favor. Idealizing an outcome or believing that we will always win creates a relationship of dependence on the environment, and when it does not meet our expectations, disappointment and frustration take over. Instead of idealizing, we must be realistic and recognize that the market is unpredictable, and that our job is to adapt to its movements, not try to control it.

Dependent relationships in trading are characterized by phrases like, "If this trade goes well, then I'll be a good trader" or "If I make X amount, then I can be happy." This type of conditional thinking creates a dependency relationship with the outcome, which is extremely damaging. When we base our self-esteem or happiness on the outcome of a trade, we are giving our power to circumstances that we cannot control. Instead of depending on the results, we should focus on the process, on being consistent, and on learning from each experience, regardless of whether the outcome is positive or negative.

Comparison and contrast also break the balance. Many times, traders fall into the trap of comparing themselves to others: "That trader has better results than me, so I am less capable" or "If they can do it, I should be able to do it too." These comparisons create excessive potential that will inevitably be balanced, and often in a way that is detrimental to us. Instead of comparing ourselves, we should focus on our own path, our own goals, and our own growth. Every trader has a different path, and the key is to respect and accept our own evolution without the need to idealize the achievements of others or devalue ourselves for not being at the same level.

All internal and external conflicts arise from comparison and contrast. When we idealize or compare, we create a tension that the equalizing forces will seek to resolve, and often this results in disappointment, conflict, or loss. In the context of trading, this can lead to poor decisions driven by the desire to achieve an idealization that is not realistic. For example, a trader might risk more than he should because he idealizes the idea of making big profits quickly, comparing himself to others who have apparently achieved this. However, this idealization only leads him to take unnecessary risks and to lose his emotional and financial balance.

To illustrate this, imagine an athlete who constantly compares himself to other competitors. If his focus is on how others perform, he will inevitably feel like he is never good enough, which leads to excessive pressure and a loss of self-confidence. The same thing happens in trading. Constantly comparing ourselves to other traders distracts us from our own learning process and pushes us to take risks that are not aligned with our trading plan. The key is to learn to focus on ourselves, on our own progress, without falling into the trap of unnecessary comparisons.

On the other hand, if we learn to view the environment and our operations in a more neutral way, without idealizing or generating excessive expectations, we can operate with a clearer mind and a calmer attitude. This does not mean being indifferent or not having aspirations, but rather staying detached from the outcome and focusing on what we can control: our preparation, our strategy and our discipline. Just as true love does not try to possess or control, the love of trading should not be based on impossible expectations or the need to prove something. We must learn to enjoy the process, to accept losses as part of the journey, and to move forward with serenity and confidence.

When we idealize a situation or an asset, we also tend to lose perspective and ignore warning signs that could help us minimize risks. For example, a trader who idealizes an asset may be reluctant to place a stop loss, thinking that the trade is guaranteed to succeed. This is a serious mistake, as no instrument is risk-free, and conditions can change dramatically at any time. Instead of idealizing, we should be disciplined and always be prepared to act rationally, without being carried away by the desire for our idealized vision to come true.

Another way to avoid dependency is through the practice of acceptance. Acceptance is not resignation, but an attitude of acknowledging reality as it is, without trying to force it to change it. In trading, this means accepting that sometimes our trades will not go as we expect, and that not everything is under our control. By accepting this reality, we can make more objective decisions and not be swept away by the negative emotions that arise from unmet expectations. Acceptance allows us to act with clarity and focus on what we can do, rather than lamenting what we cannot control.

A good exercise to foster acceptance is to keep a trading journal. In this journal, you not only record your trades, but also the emotions and expectations that accompany each decision. Over time, this allows you to identify thought patterns that lead you to idealize situations or become dependent on outcomes. Reflecting on these entries helps you adjust your mindset and take a more balanced and objective stance toward market conditions.

Finally, remember that we are all guests in this world, and in the trading arena, no one has absolute control over circumstances. We should not idealize or try to control that which is beyond our reach. Instead of creating relationships of dependence on the results, we should learn to flow with the environment, adapting to its movements and accepting both gains and losses. Imagine a river that flows naturally, overcoming obstacles without stopping. When it encounters a rock, it does not try to move it or fight it, it simply adapts, going around it and continuing its course. In the same way, we must learn to be like the river: accept obstacles without resistance and move forward. Stay calm, accept the present moment, and keep moving forward. This attitude will allow you to operate with a clear mind and a calm heart, maintaining the mental balance necessary to face the challenges and take advantage of the opportunities that arise.

In conclusion, we must learn to differentiate between love and idealization. Loving the trading process means being committed to our continuous improvement, accepting our failures and learning from them, and maintaining an attitude of constant learning. Idealization, on the other hand, leads us to depend on specific results and to generate unrealistic expectations that end up affecting our emotional well-being. The key is to stay balanced, accept what we cannot change, and focus on what is within our control. Only then will we be able to operate with clarity, confidence, and, above all, enjoy the journey that is trading without being tied to the ups and downs of the market.

Illusions and overconfidence

Overvaluation means attributing to a person, asset or strategy qualities that it does not actually possess. In the trading context, this can manifest as wishful thinking that seems harmless, but can lead to unrealistic expectations. On an energetic level, this overvaluation creates "excessive potential," which arises when there is a significant difference between reality and the idealized image we create. This potential is eventually balanced by balancing forces, and the result is often demystification and disillusionment.

It is common to see traders overhyping certain well-known figures, specific strategies, or even certain assets. Imagine a novice trader who starts following a trading "guru" who promises great returns. This trader might end up idealizing the guru, assuming that everything he says is infallible and that if he follows his advice, he will be guaranteed success. However, in due time reality sets in: the environment is unpredictable, and even the best investor makes mistakes. When the "guru" gets it wrong, disappointment is inevitable, and the idealizing trader might feel cheated, falling into frustration and resentment.

This is similar to the story of Karl May, a German writer known for his novels about the Wild West. Karl May wrote incredibly detailed and exciting stories about characters like Winnetou and Sure Hand, creating a very convincing impression that he had lived through these adventures himself. His novels were so vivid and realistic that many of his readers were convinced that May had been a real adventurer, roaming the lands of the West and taking part in countless escapades. This idealization of Karl May as a brave and experienced man created an image of him that was much larger than life.

However, the truth was very different. Karl May had never been to America when he wrote most of his novels, and in fact, some of his works were written while he was in prison for minor crimes. The demystification occurred when it was revealed that May had never set foot in the Wild West, and that his stories were the product of his imagination and his ability to research and describe places he had never been. When his admirers discovered the truth, many were deeply disappointed.

They had created an image of Karl May as a real hero, and when they discovered that he had never lived the adventures he described, that idealization crumbled, leading them to reject and even hate him. This story shows us how idealization can lead to unrealistic expectations and, eventually, to disillusionment when reality does not match those expectations.

The problem with idealization is that it creates a relationship of dependency. When we overvalue someone or something, we become dependent on that person or strategy meeting our unrealistic expectations. If it doesn't, the emotional blow can be devastating. In trading, this can mean the loss of not only capital, but also self-confidence. It's important to remember that all traders, even the most experienced, make mistakes. No strategy is foolproof, and no asset is guaranteed to always go up.

Another example of overvaluation is when a trader creates an idealized image of themselves as an "expert" who will always make the right decisions. This self-overvaluation leads the trader to make overconfident decisions, without considering the real risks. Overvaluation of our own abilities leads us to believe that we are in absolute control, which is a mistake that will inevitably be corrected by reality. Overvaluation can lead us to ignore risk management rules, underestimate negative signals, or hold on to a losing position hoping for a recovery just because we believe we can't go wrong.

Instead of idealizing, we must adopt a realistic and balanced attitude. Balance is achieved when we recognize the real qualities of a strategy, an asset or a person, without attributing imaginary qualities to it. As traders, we must focus on facts, data and evidence, not on illusions or false promises. It is essential to question everything, even those we admire or consider experts. This does not mean being cynical or distrustful, but rather maintaining a critical mindset that allows us to differentiate between reality and fantasy.

It is also important to talk about the overvaluation of certain assets. During the cryptocurrency boom, many investors idealized Bitcoin or other cryptocurrencies, believing that their value could only increase. This idealization led many to invest without considering the risks, ignoring warning signs and even holding positions when prices began to fall dramatically. History teaches us that no asset is immune to volatility, and that idealizing an asset blinds us to the inherent risks. The result of this overvaluation is often a great financial and emotional loss.

Another way overhype can manifest itself is when we build castles in the air, idealizing a future without a real foundation. A trader might imagine themselves making millions and living a life of luxury through trading, without considering the challenges and constant work involved in being profitable in this activity. This fantasy, while motivating, can become an obstacle if not complemented by a realistic action plan and constant discipline. The forces of reality will always adjust our expectations, and those who live in a constant fantasy will find themselves facing situations they were not prepared for.

To avoid falling into the trap of overvaluation, it is important to cultivate humility and acceptance of our own limitations. Trading is a continuous process of learning and improvement, and there is no room for believing that we know everything or that we are immune to mistakes. Humility allows us to learn from our failures and grow as traders. In addition, we must learn to value things for what they really are, without exaggerating their qualities. It is like appreciating a beautiful landscape without feeling the need to own it or change it; simply observing and learning from it.

A useful analogy to remember this concept is the story of fireflies in the dark. On a moonless night, fireflies emit light and impress us with their brilliance. However, their light is small and fleeting compared to daylight. If we idealize a firefly, we might think it is the most important source of light, but when the sun comes up, we realize that it was just a small spark in the darkness. We should not idealize those small sparks of success or the "gurus" who shine momentarily; we should keep perspective and understand that the environment is complex and much larger than any individual figure or specific strategy.

Another analogy that can help us understand this concept is the story of Icarus in Greek mythology. Icarus, dazzled by the idea of flying close to the sun with his wings made of wax and feathers, ignored his father's warnings and got carried away by the enthusiasm of his ability to fly. But when he got too close to the sun, the wax on his wings melted, and he ended up falling into the sea. This story reminds us of the importance of not getting carried away by excessive enthusiasm or overestimating our abilities. Flying too high without recognizing the risks can have very negative consequences. We must be cautious and recognize the limits that exist, without falling into the trap of believing that we are invincible.

In trading, it is easy to fall into the trap of idealizing certain moments of success and thinking that they will always happen again. A common example is when a trader has a streak of successful trades and begins to think that they have mastered trading. This idealization of past success leads to overconfidence, which can result in large losses. The environment is changing and every situation is unique. Idealizing a past result without considering current conditions is a mistake that can be costly. The key is to understand that every trade is different and success is not guaranteed simply by having been successful before. Humility and constant preparation are essential to prevent unrealistic expectations from leading us to make wrong decisions.

Another important aspect to consider is the overvaluation of a single strategy. Many traders, after experiencing success with a specific strategy, tend to idealize it and blindly trust that it will always work. However, conditions change and what works today might not work tomorrow. A trader who overvalues a strategy may ignore the signs that conditions have changed, remaining rigid and unadaptable. Adaptability is one of the most important qualities of a good trader, and overvaluing a single way of trading can be a barrier to this necessary flexibility. It is essential to always be willing to evaluate our strategies and adjust them according to the conditions.

Instead of idealizing, we need to adopt an attitude of constant curiosity. This means that instead of assuming we know everything there is to know about a strategy, a well-known figure, or an asset, we should be willing to continually learn and question our assumptions. Curiosity keeps us open to new opportunities and allows us to better adapt to changes in the environment. Instead of blindly trusting a strategy, we can try different approaches, analyze the results, and adapt based on what is working best at the moment.

A practical way to avoid overhyping is to keep a detailed record of our trades and our emotions along the way. By reviewing our trading journal, we can identify when we are idealizing an asset, a strategy, or our own skills. By being aware of these thought patterns, we can actively work to correct them and adopt a more balanced perspective. A trading journal not only helps us strengthen our technical skills, but it is also a powerful tool to develop a more realistic and objective mindset, thus avoiding the trap of idealization.

Finally, it is essential to remember that trading is a complex discipline that requires emotional balance, humility and a critical mindset. Idealization and overvaluation in trading lead to unrealistic expectations and dependency relationships that are damaging both emotionally and financially. It is crucial to maintain a realistic mindset, question our beliefs and not attribute imaginary qualities to people, assets or strategies. Loving the process of trading involves accepting the uncertainty and unpredictability of this activity, and learning to operate without relying on false promises or illusions. Only then will we be able to navigate this environment with clarity, confidence and balance, truly taking advantage of the opportunities that arise without losing sight of reality. Let us always remember that trading is a journey of continuous learning and that we must be willing to adapt and evolve, without falling into the trap of idealizing either ourselves or others.

Judgments and Arrogance

Judging other people is one of the most common ways we upset the balance in life. In the context of trading, this type of judgment can also lead to negative consequences. Looking down on other traders, thinking we are superior, or seeing others' strategies as worthless, is a dangerous path that can lead to costly mistakes. As in other areas of life, contempt and vanity in trading throw us off the balance needed to thrive.

On the energetic level, there are no good or bad people; there are only those who align themselves with natural laws and those who, through their judgments and actions, cause disorder in the "status quo." This disorder will eventually attract forces that will seek to restore the lost balance. In the context of trading, these forces manifest when our attitudes of contempt or vanity lead us to miss opportunities or suffer the consequences of the financial environment. Energy within the trading sphere tends to correct excesses of arrogance and unfair judgments, since any imbalance generates a reaction that seeks to restore harmony.

An example of this is when a trader looks down on others for being too conservative. He may think that his own aggressive style is superior and that those who take less risk are simply "scared." However, the financial environment is unpredictable, and a conservative strategy may be the one that survives a major downturn in economic conditions, while the trader who looked down on this strategy ends up losing a large portion of his capital. In this case, the forces of the system restore balance, showing that disdain and arrogance have no place in such a volatile arena as trading. In fact, the financial system has a peculiar way of humiliating even the most confident. Traders who ignore the importance of conservative strategies often face a harsh lesson in the relevance of risk management and prudence.

Disdain can also manifest itself towards certain assets or strategies. Some traders may consider strategies such as buy and hold to be ineffective or inferior compared to day trading. This attitude can lead them to lose sight of the advantages that a long-term strategy could offer, especially during periods of high volatility. The dynamics of the financial environment tends to act in a way that makes us reconsider our beliefs and prejudices, and often they do so in the harshest way possible: by hitting our capital and our emotions. Ignoring the benefits of a long-term strategy, believing that day trading is the only way to make a profit, can result in lost opportunities and, worse still, significant financial losses.

Another manifestation of imbalance is vanity. There is nothing wrong with feeling proud of one's own achievements, as long as that pride does not cause us to underestimate others or overvalue our capabilities. Vanity becomes a problem when we begin to believe that we will always make the right decisions and that our skills will make us immune to losses. This mindset can be particularly dangerous after a series of successful trades when the trader begins to feel invincible. Vanity creates excessive potential that eventually attracts consequences in the environment that restore balance. This adjustment often comes in the form of a significant loss that reminds the investor that no one is infallible.

Imagine a trader who, after several successful trades, begins to think that he has a "golden touch" and that conditions will always work in his favor. That overconfidence leads him to increase his positions and take on more risks than he should. Eventually, circumstances change unexpectedly, and the investor loses much of his profits, if not all of his capital. This is the classic example of how vanity and overconfidence lead us to ignore risks and lose emotional and financial balance. This type of experience is more common than one might think, and the financial environment has a relentless way of reminding us that humility is essential for survival.

It is also important to understand how judging other traders can create excessive potential to backfire. For example, if you criticize other traders for their mistakes, you might find yourself making the same mistakes soon after. The dynamics of trading have a way of showing us that no one is above the challenges and difficulties of trading. So, instead of judging, it is better to learn from the experiences of others, both their successes and their failures. Every mistake made by another trader is an opportunity to reflect on our own decisions and avoid falling into the same traps.

An analogy that can help to understand this concept is that of a tightrope walker walking on a tightrope. Imagine that, while crossing, the tightrope walker begins to look down on those watching him from below, thinking that none of them could do what he does. This attitude of contempt distracts him from his main task: maintaining mental balance. When he loses focus, his steps falter, and he runs the risk of falling. In trading, balance is crucial, and any attitude that diverts us from our focus—such as contempt or vanity—puts us at risk of losing our way and our investments. Contempt not only distracts us, but also prevents us from learning and adapting to the fluctuations inherent in this activity.

Another example that can illustrate how the dynamics of the environment restore balance is that of traders who look down on novices. They may consider themselves experts and think that new investors are incapable of reaching their level. However, this attitude of superiority can prevent them from seeing mistakes that they themselves are making, while a novice, with his fresh and unprejudiced approach, might spot opportunities that the expert trader misses. In this way, contempt for others becomes a barrier that prevents us from learning and improving. Traders who maintain a humble attitude and are willing to learn from even the most inexperienced often find that they can see trading from a new perspective and find innovative solutions.

Vanity can take many forms, such as thinking you are always right, ignoring signals from the environment, or taking unnecessary risks because we believe we are invincible. A clear example of this is the trader who, after several months of success, decides to abandon his risk management strategy because he feels he no longer needs it. The reality of the financial field, on the other hand, is that moments of success can be fleeting, and we must always be prepared for the unexpected. Abandoning a risk management strategy out of vanity is one of the quickest ways to lose everything. The key to avoiding falling into this trap is to always remember that the conditions are bigger than any individual, and that humility and discipline are essential to staying afloat.

To avoid falling into contempt and vanity, it is essential to cultivate humility and respect for other traders, regardless of their level of experience or their strategies. Every trader has their own path and style, and we are all constantly learning. Instead of judging, we should seek to learn from others and be willing to acknowledge that we are not always right. The trading world is a great teacher who has unexpected ways of reminding us that there is always something more to learn. Even the most experienced traders encounter new situations that challenge their prior knowledge. The ability to accept uncertainty and constant change is what differentiates a successful trader from one who eventually fails.

Healthy self-love also plays an important role in keeping us balanced. Being proud of our achievements is natural, but it should be a pride based on the acceptance of our strengths and weaknesses, without the need to belittle others. When pride turns into vanity, circumstances will take care of teaching us a lesson. Therefore, we must focus on growing, not on comparing ourselves or underestimating others. Also, we must remember that success in trading is not measured by a single moment or a streak of successful trades, but by our ability to remain consistent and resilient over time.

Another aspect to consider is how the environment in which we operate can influence our attitude towards others. It is common in trading communities to have implicit competition, where traders feel the need to prove that they are better than others. This dynamic can foster contempt and vanity if not managed properly. It is important to remember that the goal of trading is not to compete against others, but to expand our own skills and achieve our personal goals. Every trader has a different style and approach, and what works for one may not work for another. Rather than seeing others as competition, it is more beneficial to see them as learning partners.

In conclusion, contempt and vanity are attitudes that misalign us from the balance necessary to be successful. These attitudes generate excessive potential that will inevitably attract forces seeking to restore harmony. In this context, this translates into losses, missed opportunities and lessons that are difficult to assimilate. The key is to cultivate humility, maintain an attitude of constant learning, and remember that we are all in a process of evolution. Each operator, regardless of their experience, has something to teach and something to learn, and only by respecting that process can we achieve a balance that allows us to prosper in this field.

Finally, we must remember that trading is a journey of self-discovery. Through our victories and defeats, we can learn a lot about who we really are. Vanity and self-deprecation not only keep us from financial success, but also prevent us from growing as people. By recognizing our limitations, learning from our mistakes, and staying humble in the face of circumstances, we can evolve not only as traders, but also as individuals. True success in trading is not found solely in profits, but in the ability to adapt, learn, and stay balanced along a path full of challenges and learnings. Every challenge we face offers us an opportunity for reflection and improvement, and every lesson, whether it comes from a victory or a defeat, brings us one step closer to maturity and resilience. Ultimately, trading is a practice that teaches us as much about the world of finance as it does about our own nature, revealing our strengths and weaknesses, and helping us build a mindset that allows us to thrive not only in the financial realm, but also in life.

Comparisons and mentality

Feelings of superiority or inferiority are a common trap for many traders and represent a form of dependency that distances us from the balance necessary to operate with clarity. In the trading field, constant comparison with others and the desire to stand out from others can generate excessive potential that ends up harming us. These feelings are merely illusory and, instead of driving us forward, they keep us trapped in a cycle of dependency and energy drain.

Imagine a trader who constantly feels superior to others because his strategies have given him positive results over time. This trader may develop an arrogant attitude, believing that his skills make him better than others and that he will always be able to overcome any challenge. This attitude of superiority leads him to take unnecessary risks, confident that he has absolute control of the situation. However, the environment is unpredictable, and eventually, such excessive confidence will meet reality. The forces that seek to balance any imbalance will act against that arrogant attitude, and the trader could face great losses that return him to humility. The lesson here is clear: in trading, arrogance and a sense of superiority have no place, as circumstances always find a way to restore balance.

The self-important investor may even begin to ignore basic risk management principles, believing that his skills protect him from adverse outcomes. This illusion of invincibility can lead him to trade with excessive leverage or hold losing positions for longer than is advisable, hoping that everything will move in his favor. The reality is that trading is a ruthless master that does not forgive arrogance, and when a correction comes, it is often devastating. Not only does this type of experience lead to significant financial losses, but it can also have a deep emotional impact, affecting the investor's confidence and leading him to a state of doubt and insecurity.

On the other hand, the feeling of inferiority is equally harmful. A trader who feels less capable than others might constantly doubt his decisions, which leads him to miss opportunities or make wrong decisions simply due to a lack of confidence. This inferiority complex is fueled by constant comparison with traders who seem more successful or experienced.

By comparing himself and feeling inferior, this trader generates excessive potential that leads him to trade with fear and anxiety, two emotions that cloud judgment and make it difficult to make good decisions. As with superiority, the feeling of inferiority generates a relationship of dependence, in this case with the perception of the abilities of others, which leaves him trapped in a position of weakness.

The trader who feels inferior can get caught in a cycle of indecision and procrastination. He may avoid executing trades, even when the signals are clear, for fear of making mistakes. This constant fear paralyzes him and, instead of taking advantage of opportunities, he sits on the sidelines, watching others get results while he feels increasingly incapable.

This lack of confidence can also lead him to rely excessively on the opinions of others, blindly following supposed experts without developing his own analytical skills. As a result, his trading decisions are inauthentic and lack conviction, making him more vulnerable to losses and frustrations.

It is important to understand that comparing yourself to others, whether to feel superior or inferior, has no real value in the context of trading. Every trader has his or her own path, style and pace of learning. Comparing yourself to others is like a fly hitting a glass, trying to get through when, next door, there is a window open. Instead of wasting energy on maintaining these excessive potentials, it is much more productive to focus on personal development, learning and elevating our own skills without worrying about how we rank against others. Trading is a deeply personal activity, and success depends more on our ability to manage our own emotions and decisions than on how we compare to others.

Energy should be directed towards self-improvement and discipline. When we stop comparing ourselves to others, we free up a wealth of energy that we can use to improve our strategies, learn new techniques, and, above all, trade with a clear and balanced mind. Traders who focus on their own growth, without worrying about being better or worse than others, often find greater success and satisfaction, as their energy is not wasted on maintaining an illusory image of superiority or trying to compensate for a feeling of inferiority. Furthermore, by focusing on their own progress, traders can identify their areas for improvement more accurately and work on them consistently and effectively.

To break free from these feelings of superiority and inferiority, it is essential to stop seeking external validation. The environment does not reward those who feel superior or punish those who feel inferior; it simply responds to our actions objectively. When we accept that we do not need to compare ourselves to others and that our value does not depend on how others perceive us, we can operate with greater freedom and confidence. This does not mean that we should ignore our weaknesses, but that we should recognize them without judgment, using them as opportunities for improvement and not as reasons to feel inferior. True growth in trading comes from the ability to be honest with ourselves, accept our limitations and work to overcome them, without falling into the trap of constant comparison.

Another important aspect is to understand that the perception of superiority or inferiority is a mental construct that limits us. Many traders, especially those starting out, can feel intimidated by the experience of others and fall into the trap of believing they will never measure up. This mindset can become a huge obstacle to learning and growth. Likewise, those who have initial success may feel they no longer need to learn more, which makes them vulnerable to mistakes that could have been avoided with a more humble attitude. The "I already know everything" mindset is dangerous because it closes us off to new learning opportunities and leaves us stagnant. Constant evolution is essential, and those who stop learning eventually fall behind.

The key to avoiding these traps is to focus on your own process and constant development. Every trade is an opportunity to learn, regardless of whether it results in a profit or a loss. Instead of comparing ourselves to others, we should compare our current actions to our past actions, always seeking to improve. The real competition is not about being better than other traders, but about being better than the trader we were yesterday. This involves developing our technical skills, improving our discipline, and learning to manage our emotions more effectively. By focusing on our own growth, we can move forward at our own pace, without the unnecessary pressure of competing with the achievements of others.

Finally, giving up the need to feel superior does not mean humiliating yourself. Humility does not mean underestimating our capabilities, but rather recognizing them as they are, without the need to prove anything to anyone. Like the feeling of superiority, the feeling of inferiority is also a distortion that generates harmful potentials. Instead of fighting against our imperfections, we can work to compensate for them with other qualities and focus our energy on self-development. Only by freeing ourselves from the burden of constantly comparing ourselves to others can we reach a state of balance that allows us to thrive both in trading and in life.

True freedom comes from trading without the need to impress others or feel less than someone else. When we let go of comparison, we can focus on what really matters: our own progress and our own goals. Humility allows us to accept losses without feeling like failures and celebrate wins without feeling invincible. Emotional balance is the key to surviving and thriving in trading, and this balance is only achieved when we free ourselves from the chains of superiority and inferiority. At the end of the day, the goal is not to be better than anyone else, but to be the best version of ourselves.

In the world of trading, the intense desire to obtain something or to avoid something can become a significant obstacle to achieving success. Both greed and fear, which are extreme forms of desire, create what we might call "excessive potential" that upsets a trader's emotional balance and distances him from making rational decisions. In this text, we explore how the strength of our desires can interfere with our performance and how learning to manage these desires can lead us to a better balance and, therefore, better results.

Imagine a trader who is obsessed with making a large amount of money in a short period of time. His desire to make a profit is so intense that he decides to gamble everything on a single trade, ignoring his risk management plan. This trader is unwittingly creating excessive potential that will harm him. The desperate need to win causes him to make impulsive decisions and, in the end, when circumstances move against his trade, his loss is not only financial, but also emotional. The lesson here is clear: the more you obsess about obtaining a specific result, the harder it becomes to achieve it, as that obsession distorts your judgment and leads you to make mistakes.

We can highlight three main ways in which desire manifests itself. The first way is when desire becomes a firm intention and is translated into action. In this case, the investor has a clear goal, but is not emotionally attached to that goal; he simply takes the actions necessary to achieve it, such as planning his trade, following his strategy, and executing with discipline. Here, the energy of desire is used constructively and not wasted.

The second way is when desire is not translated into action, but remains a constant concern. The trader wants to be successful, but does not take concrete steps to achieve it, which creates excessive potential that only generates anxiety and burnout. The third way, the most dangerous, is when desire becomes a dependence on the result: "I must win this trade, otherwise my career as an investor is pointless" or "I need to win, so I can pay the rent on my apartment." This dependence creates a harmful relationship with the environment and leads the trader into a spiral of frustration and disappointment.

A trader who is emotionally dependent on a specific outcome is like someone trying to catch a bird in the woods. The more desperate the hunter is, growling and making noise in his eagerness to catch the bird, the further away the bird will go. However, if the hunter walks calmly through the woods without showing anxiety, the bird may come closer. The same is true in trading: the stronger the desire to win and the need for conditions to move in your favor, the more likely the opposite is to happen, as decisions driven by anxiety often lead to mistakes.

Desire also has another side: the desire to avoid losses. This desire is a logical continuation of fear, and the more we try to avoid a situation, the more we confront it. A trader who is afraid of losing might close his trades too early, securing small profits but missing out on big opportunities. Or worse, he might avoid entering a trade when the signal is clear, due to the fear of being wrong. Such behavior not only affects performance, but also creates excessive potential that, instead of protecting the investor, puts him in unfavorable situations. When the desire to avoid losses is too strong, circumstances often find ways to show the trader that he does not have absolute control, increasing the frequency of adverse situations.

It is essential to learn to lower the level of importance we give to each operation. If we see each operation as something that will define our success or failure, we are creating an emotional burden that will prevent us from acting clearly. Instead, we must treat each operation neutrally, as another process within our overall strategy.

The best way to trade is with pure intention: having a clear objective, but without being attached to it. A good example of this is imagining that you are going to the supermarket to buy a bottle of water. You do not obsess about whether the bottle of water will be available or not; you simply act intending to buying it and, if you cannot do so, you choose another brand or go somewhere else to buy it. Applying this mentality to trading allows us to trade without creating excessive potentials, which helps us stay balanced and make rational decisions.

The strong desire to make a profit or avoid a loss is also related to confidence. When a trader clings to the idea of winning because he feels it is the only way to validate his ability, he is demonstrating a lack of confidence in his process and strategy. The emission of energy of this type is transmitted with "interference", as deep down the trader does not fully believe in the realization of his desire. Trying with all his might that conditions will move in his favor only creates more anxiety and increases overpotential. Instead of focusing on the outcome, it is more effective to focus on the process: making sure to follow good risk management, analyze the signals correctly, and execute the trade as planned. In this way, the desire becomes a balanced intention and the trader operates from a state of calm and clarity.

To achieve success, it is essential to reduce the importance we give to each individual outcome. This does not mean being indifferent, but rather learning to treat each operation with its fair value, without exaggerating its importance. The environment in which we operate is neutral, it has no emotions or intentions; it simply responds to our actions. By reducing our emotional dependence on the outcome of a trade, we can operate with pure intention and free of excessive potentials, allowing us to better align ourselves with real conditions. The key is to act consistently, without allowing greed or fear to dictate our decisions.

Ultimately, true freedom in trading comes from trading without being tied down by the intense desire to win or the fear of losing. When we learn to treat each trade as another step in our path of learning and development, we can release the energy that was previously trapped in extreme worries and emotions. This freed energy can be used to strengthen our skills, fine-tune our strategies, and, above all, enjoy the trading process without the constant burden of anxiety. The goal is not to always win, but to trade in a way that allows us to continue learning and growing, both as traders and as individuals.

For many traders, the key to success lies in cultivating a mindset of growth and continuous learning. This means accepting that every trade, whether a winner or a loser, is an opportunity to learn something new.

Instead of viewing losses as personal failures, we can interpret them as part of the natural process of trading. Conditions are constantly changing, and the ability to adapt to those changes is what allows us to evolve and thrive. When we detach ourselves from the intense desire to succeed at all costs and accept that success is a journey full of ups and downs, we become more resilient, able to face challenges with a more flexible and positive mindset. Instead of feeling defeated by every obstacle, we learn to view them as opportunities to grow and improve, which ultimately makes us stronger and more consistent traders.

Feeling of guilt

Guilt is excessive potential in its purest form and can have a significant impact on a trader's performance. In the nature of the market, there are no concepts such as right or wrong; price movements have no morals, they are merely a consequence of forces operating without emotions of their own. However, traders often interpret their actions through the lens of personal judgment, which creates emotional baggage that interferes with their ability to trade rationally. This personal judgment can cause a trader to focus on what they did wrong, rather than what they can learn from the situation, which is counterproductive to developing a resilient and effective trading mindset.

After a failed trade, a trader may experience a feeling of guilt, thinking that he did not make a good decision, that he did not follow his plan properly, or that he should have acted differently. This feeling of guilt creates excessive potential in his emotional field that eventually translates into counterproductive behaviors, such as overtrading, lack of confidence to enter the market, or even the inability to accept losses and exit a trade in time. Guilt prevents the trader from seeing the loss as a lesson and instead perceives it as a personal failure, contributing to a vicious cycle of impulsive and poorly managed decisions.

Guilt can create a self-imposed cycle of punishment. Imagine a trader who loses a significant amount of money because he acted impulsively. Instead of accepting the loss as part of the process and learning from it, he feels guilty. That guilt leads him to want to redeem himself quickly, seeking to "recover" what he lost, which pushes him to take bigger risks or enter trades without proper analysis. This cycle of guilt and punishment not only increases the risk of further losses, but also negatively affects the trader's emotional balance. Furthermore, guilt can affect a trader's ability to maintain discipline, as the desire to correct a past mistake can lead him to bypass his own trading plan and act from desperation instead of logic.

This cycle can be very difficult to break because guilt fuels the need to perform perfectly. However, perfection in trading does not exist. All traders, even the most experienced, make mistakes. What distinguishes successful investors is their ability to learn from those mistakes without getting caught up in guilt. Trading requires a mindset in which mistakes are seen as opportunities to improve, not reasons to beat yourself up. In this sense, breaking guilt involves understanding that every loss is an investment in experience, and that every failed trade can offer valuable lessons for the future.

Another way guilt manifests itself is through guilt induced by social pressure. Traders are often exposed to the opinions of analysts, mentors, colleagues, or even the trading community on social media. When a trader decides contrary to what the "experts" recommend and ends up losing, he or she may feel even greater guilt, as he or she is not only dealing with the loss, but also with the feeling of having defied what others considered right. This external pressure can cause the trader to doubt his or her own abilities, which increases insecurity and the likelihood of making more mistakes.

Manipulators can be those voices that try to make you feel guilty for not following their recommendations or for not performing according to their expectations. These manipulators often base their influence on the trust that other traders place in them, taking advantage of any mistake to make others feel inadequate or incapable. The best way to avoid falling under this influence is to give up the feeling of guilt and trust your own process. If you do not consider yourself guilty of a failed trade, no outside opinion will have power over you, and you will be able to learn from your mistakes without carrying unnecessary emotional weight. Developing confidence in your own judgment and process is essential to maintaining mental independence and avoiding being swept away by the pressure of others.

Guilt brings nothing useful or constructive to trading. It doesn't help you improve or solve problems; on the contrary, it only creates more tension and distorts decision-making. The best course of action is to prevent situations that lead to guilt, and if we are already trapped in it, it is important to let go of it as soon as possible. Remember that every trade is a lesson, and every mistake has the potential to teach you something valuable. Instead of considering a loss as a failure, see it as an opportunity to learn what aspects of your strategy need adjusting.

Instead of focusing on what you did wrong, focus on what you could do better next time. Keeping a trading journal can be a compelling tool for this purpose. By recording every trade, including the reasons behind each decision and the results achieved, you can objectively analyze your mistakes without judgment or blame. This allows you to view trading as a process of continuous improvement, where there is no ultimate success or failure, but rather constant learning. A trading journal also allows you to identify patterns of behavior that lead to mistakes, and once those patterns are identified, you can actively work to change them.

Another powerful tool for letting go of guilt is the practice of self-acceptance. Accept that you will make mistakes and that losses are an inevitable part of trading. By accepting this, you can significantly reduce the emotional burden that accompanies a failed trade. Self-acceptance helps you view each mistake as a natural part of the process, not a personal failing that needs to be punished. Over time, this attitude will allow you to trade with a calmer, more centered mindset, focusing on the process rather than individual outcomes.

In the trading world, those who achieve greater emotional stability are those who have less guilt in their hearts. The absence of guilt grants independence and security, two essential qualities for any investor. If a trader accepts the possibility of losing as part of the process and does not feel guilty about it, he or she will be able to act with greater confidence and without fear of punishment. This courage does not mean being reckless, but rather operating from a state of mind in which there is no room for self-condemnation, only for learning. The confidence that comes from the absence of guilt allows the investor to stay true to his or her plan and avoid impulsive decisions that arise from fear or desperation.

On the other hand, the tactic of asking for forgiveness can also be useful, but in an internal way. Asking for forgiveness from yourself for a loss or a mistake can help you release the accumulated tension and avoid carrying that excessive potential that affects your future decisions. On the other hand, you must make sure not to turn this into a habit that leads to complacency. Acknowledge the mistake, learn from it, ask for forgiveness and move on without looking back. The goal is to release the emotional burden, not to justify undisciplined behavior.

Giving up the feeling of guilt is one of the keys to surviving in the emotionally challenging trading environment. The true strength of an investor lies not in the ability to consistently make profits, but in the ability to learn, adapt, and trade without the emotional burdens that can affect their judgment. If you allow yourself to be yourself, accepting both your successes and your mistakes, the fear of punishment dissipates and you can trade with a clear and calm mind. In this way, you put yourself in a position where decisions are made based on the reality of the market and not on accumulated negative emotions. This attitude not only improves the quality of your decisions, but also helps you build a sustainable and rewarding trading career.

Trading, at its core, is a game of chance where you don't always win, but every experience counts. The ability to trade without guilt, to accept losses and see them as part of the process, is what makes the difference between those who thrive and those who are stuck in a cycle of frustration. Letting go of guilt doesn't mean you stop worrying; it means worrying in the right way: learning, adapting, and moving forward. Instead of beating yourself up for every mistake, turn them into learning opportunities that allow you to grow and evolve as a trader. This mindset will help you stay positive, maintain mental clarity, and ultimately become a more consistent and successful trader.

True success in trading comes not from avoiding losses, but from learning how to manage them and continue moving forward without the emotional burdens that could destabilize your performance. Resilience, the ability to adapt, and the willingness to learn from each experience are the qualities that build a winning trader. Every trade, whether winning or losing, is a step forward on the path to mastery. Freeing yourself from guilt will allow you to make the most of each step and move forward with confidence towards the success you seek.

|"Far from learning to win, we must learn to lose."

The relationship with money

Money in trading is a fundamental issue that goes far beyond how to make quick or large profits. The way an investor relates to money directly affects his ability to make objective decisions and, therefore, his long-term success. In this sense, money should not be seen as the only objective, but as a tool that accompanies the process of operating in the markets, helping the trader to achieve more significant goals.

In the nature of trading, the concepts of "right" or "wrong" do not exist. The market has no morality; it only reflects the forces of supply and demand, reacting to the actions of participants. However, many traders fall into the trap of interpreting money from an emotional perspective, creating a burden that distorts their decisions. This emotional burden manifests itself in the form of dependence on money, an excessive desire to earn it, or a paralyzing fear of losing it, which creates a negative cycle that affects their performance and emotional stability.

The over-driven desire to make money can lead traders to trade in desperation, trying to force results. This approach is not only ineffective, but also exhausting. The mindset that money is the most important thing in every trade creates tension, and this tension can lead to costly mistakes. Emotional balance is critical, and reducing the importance given to money is key to achieving this balance. Money needs to be viewed as a natural outcome of a well-executed process, rather than a goal in itself.

One of the most important lessons for a trader is to reduce the importance of money. When too much importance is placed on it, excessive potentials are created that negatively affect performance. Emotional dependence on money can lead to behaviors such as overtrading in an attempt to quickly recoup losses, entering trades with too much risk, or avoiding valuable opportunities for fear of further losses. These behaviors tend to lead the trader into a cycle of bad decisions that increase losses and frustration.

For example, after a series of losses, a trader might develop a "bounce back" mindset, where every trade is made intending to get back to break even as quickly as possible. This approach, however, only creates greater emotional strain, leading to impulsive decisions and a greater likelihood of making mistakes. The best way to avoid this is to think of money as a means, not the end in itself. Adopting a mindset that views money as a tool, rather than an end goal, reduces the emotional burden felt with every trade.

The trader must adopt a mindset where money is seen as a tool to achieve his or her life goals, not as the only goal. This means that the trader must focus on developing skills, improving his or her strategy, and executing his or her plans consistently, rather than focusing solely on monetary gains or losses. When trading with a detached mindset, without the constant need to win or the constant fear of losing, the pressure is reduced and the ability to follow the trading plan in a disciplined manner is increased.

Detachment from money also allows the trader to make more rational decisions, as it removes the burden of having to prove something with every trade. This mindset creates a calmer, more controlled way of acting, which is essential for success in the markets. Traders who have managed to operate with this level of detachment tend to be more consistent, as their decisions are not influenced by fear or euphoria of the moment.

Reducing the importance of money does not mean being indifferent or irresponsible with it, but understanding that money is just a consequence of the process. This helps to free the trader from the constant pressure of wanting to win on every trade, allowing the focus to be directed towards the quality of decisions and execution, which are the factors that really determine long-term success.

Real goals vs. imposed goals

A common mistake traders make is to focus solely on how to make money without having a clear goal of why they want it. Trading is most effective when you have a greater purpose than just accumulating wealth. Ask yourself, what is your real goal? It could be achieving financial freedom to spend more time with family, traveling the world, or having the ability to support causes you care about. Having a clear and meaningful goal helps you reduce the importance you place on money in each trade, which contributes to better decision-making.

Many traders set goals like "make X amount of dollars per month," but these goals become artificial surrogates that create unnecessary emotional baggage. Instead, it's more effective to focus on goals that are within your control, such as improving your consistency in following your trading plan, perfecting your risk management, or correctly executing your strategy.

Having process-based goals, rather than monetary goals, allows a trader to focus on what they can directly control, which improves the quality of decisions and the ability to maintain discipline.

When you focus on the process and not the monetary outcome, you allow yourself to trade with less stress and more clarity. The irony of trading is that by reducing the importance of money and focusing on the process, your financial results naturally improve. By taking a long-term view and valuing progress over immediate money, you build a solid foundation for sustainability and satisfaction in trading.

Traders who manage to adopt real, personal goals rather than goals imposed by the environment find greater satisfaction and balance. By having meaningful goals, investors develop emotional resilience that allows them to calmly face the ups and downs of the industry, as their sense of success does not depend on each individual trade, but on progress toward a larger purpose. This not only contributes to emotional well-being, but also improves the ability to maintain discipline and objectivity.

Money flow is an important concept to maintain emotional harmony. Instead of holding on to every dollar and fearing loss, the investor must understand that money is constantly in motion and taking risks is part of the process. Trading is not about avoiding every possible loss, but about managing risk and allowing capital to flow, accepting both gains and losses in a balanced manner.

When money stagnates or any loss is avoided at all costs, excessive potential is generated, which can manifest itself in decision paralysis or inability to act when good opportunities arise. By holding on to money too much and not allowing themselves to take risks, the trader loses the ability to adapt to circumstances and becomes a victim of their own fears.

A trader who is paralyzed by the fear of losing money or who avoids making decisions for fear of making mistakes creates a barrier to growth. Trading should be viewed as a constant flow, where losses and gains are natural parts of the process. Trades should be made with the acceptance that losses are inevitable and part of the game. By allowing yourself to trade freely, without the constant fear of losing, you become more aligned with the environment and can react to its movements more effectively.

The idea that money should also flow implies a mindset of generosity towards oneself and towards the process. This means not beating yourself up for losses and not obsessing over profits. The trader must understand that while profits are important, they should not be the only measure of their success. Every trade is an opportunity to learn, and that learning has a value that is not always reflected in the bank account, but is crucial to long-term success.

Allowing money to flow also means being willing to invest in yourself and your development as a trader. Investing in education, analytical tools, or even the rest needed to maintain good mental health are ways to ensure that the flow of money is also aligned with personal and professional growth. When the investor understands that money is a tool that can be used to improve, and not just a resource to accumulate, they begin to build a healthier and more productive relationship with it.

Money in trading should be seen as a means, not an end. The excessive importance given to money creates an emotional burden that interferes with a trader's ability to make objective decisions. Instead of focusing on the amount of money won or lost, the investor should concentrate on the process: on expanding their skills, maintaining discipline, and executing their plan consistently.

The key is to reduce the importance of money, focus on personal goals beyond money, and allow money to flow naturally. By adopting a more detached mindset, the trader can operate with more clarity, make better decisions, and build a more sustainable and rewarding trading career. Trading from a place of confidence, without fear of punishment or loss, frees the investor to act in a way that is aligned with their goals and take advantage of the opportunities that arise without the pressure of constantly having to prove something.

Trading is not a quick path to riches, but rather a process of continuous learning and personal growth. By redefining your relationship with money, seeing losses as part of the journey and focusing on the process rather than the outcome, you open the door to developing a resilient and effective mindset, capable of facing challenges calmly and confidently. This attitude is what truly differentiates successful traders from those who will be stuck in the cycle of frustration and despair.

The trader who learns to go with the flow of money, who understands that both losses and gains are inevitable parts of the process, and who chooses to focus on developing his skills and the learning process, is the one who ends up building a path to true financial freedom. This freedom is not measured only in terms of wealth accumulation, but in the ability to operate without the chains of emotional pressure, fear of failure, or the need for constant validation. In the end, true success lies in the ability to stay balanced, learn from each experience, and enjoy the process of continuous growth.

The Trap of Perfection in Trading

The quest for perfection can become a dangerous trap. Many traders fall into the mindset that they must perform every trade flawlessly, without errors. This need to be perfect not only creates unnecessary emotional drain, but can also seriously harm their performance in the financial arena. In the nature of trading, there is no such thing as absolute perfection; there is always a degree of uncertainty that must be accepted and managed in the best possible way. The idea that one can have perfect control over every aspect of a trade is actually an illusion that leads the investor to fight against themselves and against the reality of the environment.

The intention to do everything right is not bad in itself, but when it becomes an obsession, it can create enormous internal pressure that distorts a trader's judgment. This pressure often manifests itself in a constant search for the perfect strategy, the perfect entry, or the ideal time to trade. However, in trading, there is no one time or strategy that guarantees absolute success.

Every trade involves risks and opportunities, and the key is to manage those risks and learn from each experience, rather than trying to eliminate any possibility of error.

When a trader becomes obsessed with perfection, he or she enters into a detrimental cycle: he or she tries to be flawless on every trade, but inevitably encounters mistakes and adverse results, which increases frustration. This frustration leads him or her to strive even harder to be perfect, which only increases the pressure and creates more mistakes. It is a self-reinforcing cycle that can lead a trader to question his or her abilities and even to quit trading. The constant pursuit of perfection becomes an invisible enemy that sabotages every attempt at improvement.

A trader who insists on always finding the perfect entry may end up missing out on valuable opportunities due to over-analysis. This situation, known as "analysis paralysis," occurs when so much time is spent assessing and re-assessing market conditions that, in the end, the ideal moment to enter has already passed. This obsessive need to avoid mistakes leads the trader to inaction, which is also a form of error, since in trading, timing and action are of the essence. Furthermore, this inaction can trigger a feeling of frustration and hopelessness that affects the trader's confidence, creating a vicious cycle that is difficult to break out of.

Another common example is traders who, when they make a mistake, focus so much on not repeating it that they end up losing the ability to adapt to new situations. Instead of learning from mistakes and moving forward, the perfectionist gets stuck in the past, reliving each mistake and analyzing every detail to find a way to avoid future failures. This attitude not only creates significant emotional drain, but also prevents the development of the mental flexibility necessary to be successful.

Accepting imperfection is one of the most important lessons a trader can learn. The reality is that no trade will ever be perfect, and there will always be variables outside our control. Rather than constantly striving for an unattainable ideal, it is more effective to adopt a mindset of continuous improvement.

This mindset allows the trader to learn from every trade, whether a winner or a loser, and use that information to improve their skills and future decisions. By accepting imperfection, the trader is relieved of the pressure of having to prove something with every trade, which contributes to a more relaxed and effective approach.

Perfectionism can also lead traders to be overly demanding of themselves and often of others. A trader who strives to be perfect might become frustrated with his or her results and start blaming market conditions, other people, or even loved ones for his or her failures. This type of attitude not only affects a trader's ability to learn, but it also poisons his or her personal relationships, creating a toxic environment both inside and outside the trading arena. It is crucial to understand that the market has no morals or personal intentions; it simply moves according to supply and demand. Blaming external factors or oneself excessively only increases frustration and reduces the ability to make objective decisions.

Continuous improvement is a healthy alternative to perfectionism. It involves recognizing that there is always room for improvement, but without the unrealistic expectation of being perfect. Instead of seeking the perfect trade, an investor who practices continuous improvement focuses on refining their strategy, adjusting their risk management, and learning from each experience, regardless of whether the outcome was positive or negative. This approach allows for constant evolution and a clearer view of what really matters: consistency and discipline.

A trader who embraces continuous improvement understands that the goal is not to avoid all losses, but to minimize their impact and maximize learning. This mindset reduces emotional pressure as the focus shifts from "I must win on every trade" to "I must trade according to my plan and learn from every outcome." By removing the burden of perfection, the trader can trade with more clarity and effectiveness, better aligning with environmental conditions. Furthermore, continuous improvement involves an open attitude toward learning, accepting that each day is an opportunity to gain new knowledge and adjust approaches as needed.

Emotional balance is key for any trader. The need to be perfect creates excessive potential, which, in energetic terms, manifests itself as a constant tension that seeks to be compensated. This tension leads to mistakes, as the trader is too focused on avoiding failure and loses the ability to adapt to circumstances.

In contrast, a balanced approach, where losses are accepted as a natural part of the process, allows the trader to remain calm and make rational decisions. Accepting imperfection not only reduces anxiety, but also improves the trader's ability to react appropriately to unexpected situations.

Perfectionism can also lead to a distorted view of trading success. For some, success means making no mistakes and always winning, but this view is unrealistic. True success lies in consistency, discipline, and the ability to stick with it for the long term. This is only possible if the investor learns to deal with imperfection and accept that every trade, whether winning or losing, is an opportunity to learn and grow. Consistency, rather than perfection, is what separates successful traders from those who give up after facing obstacles.

The pursuit of perfection is a trap that can severely limit a trader's growth. Instead of striving for perfection, a trader should focus on continuous improvement, accepting that mistakes are inevitable and that every experience, good or bad, brings value. Adopting a continuous improvement mindset allows one to reduce emotional pressure, trade with greater clarity, and develop a healthier relationship with trading. By focusing on the process rather than the outcome, a trader can find satisfaction and growth every step of the way.

The key is to accept that trading is a constant learning process and that perfection is not the goal, but progress. By letting go of the need to be perfect and embracing imperfection as part of the journey, the trader is freed from an unnecessary burden and can focus on what really matters: being consistent, disciplined, and learning from every step taken on the path to success. This mindset not only improves performance in this activity, but also contributes to a more balanced and satisfying life, where trading becomes an enriching activity and not a constant source of stress and frustration.

The trader who learns to embrace imperfection and focus on continuous progress develops a resilience that keeps him grounded in the face of environmental challenges. This resilience, combined with a mindset of constant improvement, is the true key to achieving sustainable trading success. Instead of obsessing over avoiding mistakes, the trader must view each mistake as an opportunity to grow, understanding that the true value of trading is not in avoiding risk, but in learning to navigate it effectively and consciously.

Importance is one of the greatest obstacles any trader faces, as it creates excessive potential that can unleash equipoise forces against us. To understand this concept in depth, it is helpful to first explore how importance manifests itself in everyday life, as expounded by Vadim Zeland.

Vadim Zeland explains importance in two main forms: inner weight and outer weight. Both types of importance have the power to create tension and imbalance, which triggers problems due to the intervention of balancing forces – forces that try to restore energy balance.

Inner weight

This type of importance manifest itself as an overvaluation of our own qualities or defects. A person might think, "I am someone exceptional" or "My job is critical." In these cases, the person is attributing a high value to his or her role in the world, which generates excessive potential that the forces of balance try to compensate for. This compensation can cause circumstances that "bring the individual down from the cloud," such as failure or disappointment. Likewise, inner weight also manifests itself negatively when a person underestimates and humiliates himself or herself, also generating an imbalance that translates into obstacles and setbacks.

For example, envision someone preparing to give a presentation and is convinced that it must be perfect because they feel that their worth depends on it. This belief causes anxiety and makes the person feel overexerted. Ironically, this excess pressure can result in the presentation going poorly, which is accurately the opposite of what was intended.

Outer weight

Outer weight occurs when we attribute too much significance to external circumstances. Its formula is: "This is essential to me" or "This event will determine my future." Suppose that you are crossing a log that is lying on the ground. You would probably do so without any problems because you do not attach much importance to it.

Now imagine that the same log is placed between two tall buildings. Although it is still the same log, the situation changes because the importance of not falling becomes immense, which increases the tension and the probability of making a mistake.

Another example of outer weight could be a job interview. If a person feels that getting that job is vital to their future, this excessive importance will create a lot of pressure, which could cause nerves and mistakes during the interview. Again, the excessive potential created by importance ends up harming the desired outcome.

Downplaying doesn't mean being indifferent or uncaring, but rather avoiding giving undue value to situations, qualities or achievements. In this way, we avoid creating unnecessary tensions and allow things to flow more naturally.

Importance also has a profound impact in the world of trading, where emotional management is key to success. Traders often deal with both internal and outer weight, and both can negatively affect their performance.

Inner weight in Trading

Self-importance can manifest as an overvaluation of our abilities or a need to prove something to ourselves or others. A trader might think, "I must be a successful trader to prove my worth." This mindset creates enormous pressure that affects their ability to make objective decisions. Furthermore, if the trader suffers a loss, they might take it personally, as if their value as an individual were at stake. This approach leads to a cycle of anxiety and frustration that prevents them from learning from mistakes and growing as a trader.

Another example of inner weight is when a trader holds on to an idea that he must be right on every trade. This need to be right at all costs can cause the trader to hold on to a losing position for too long, hoping that the market will turn in his favor. Not only can this attitude lead to large losses, but it also prevents the trader from developing a flexible and adaptive mindset, which is crucial to success.

Outer weight in Trading

Outer weight, on the other hand, arises when a trader places too much value on a trade or an external event. For example, he or she might think, "It is critical that this trade be successful because I need to recoup my losses," or "This financial announcement will determine my financial success." This type of approach creates stress and causes the trader to act on impulse, based on emotions rather than objective analysis. Just like the example of the tree trunk between two buildings, the more important it is for a trader that a trade turn out perfectly, the greater the likelihood of making mistakes.

Outer weight can also manifest itself when a trader places all his hope in a single indicator or analysis. This leads to an over-reliance on external tools, without considering other factors that could influence the environment. By doing this, the investor runs the risk of getting trapped in a limited view and missing valuable opportunities to adapt to changing conditions.

We often think we are doing things right, but our perception can be biased, and we make the mistake of limiting our attitude and behavior exclusively to the realm of trading. It is essential to understand that trading is a reflection of ourselves: our attitude, habits, and life in general. In a way, YOU are the business. Trading carries your essence, it is a mirror of your life.

That said, a good way to check if you are really changing your behavior and emotion patterns is to look at your personal and family relationships. One of the easiest ways is to evaluate what your relationship is like with your partner. Do you have a healthy relationship or a toxic relationship? If you have an attractive partner, you need solid self-esteem to avoid falling into self-destructive thought patterns. If you think — or someone else tells you — "my partner is very attractive, maybe I am not good enough or attractive enough," your mind will start creating scenarios that will only reinforce that belief that you are not worthy of having an attractive partner.

You might start imagining that he or she is hiding something from you or jumping to conclusions based on behaviors that you perceive as strange. This will generate doubts in your head, creating a series of mental events that will only lead you into a spiral of negative thoughts, in which everything seems to confirm your assumptions.

You are creating in your mind a result that does not yet exist, based on assumptions and rumors. How to handle these situations? Stop and reflect if you are giving it too much importance. Focus on what you can control. The only thing you have 100% control over are your thoughts. You cannot control external events or other people. All you have to do is hope for the best possible result, and if it is not favorable, do not blame yourself or sink into despair. That's life. Put your attention on what can go well and leave aside what could go wrong because in the end it is not in your hands. As Murphy's law says: "if something can go wrong, it will go wrong," but what we must do when things do not go as we expect is to accept the result and learn from it.

To achieve emotional harmony, it is essential to reduce both internal and outer weight. Rather than viewing each trade as a test of our worth or an event that will define our future, it is more helpful to adopt an attitude of curiosity and learning. Each trade is just one of many, and no single trade defines our success or failure as traders.

The goal is to trade with discipline and consistency, without being driven by the need to be perfect or the fear of losing. By reducing importance, the trader frees himself from the emotional baggage that interferes with his ability to act rationally. When excessive importance is let go, new opportunities open up to trade more effectively and ultimately enjoy the trading process without the constant burden of anxiety and stress.

A practical strategy for reducing importance is to focus on the process rather than the outcome of each trade. This means establishing a clear trading plan and following it with discipline, regardless of whether a trade turns out to be a winner or a loser. By focusing attention on the execution of the plan and continuous learning, the trader reduces the pressure on each individual outcome and focuses on improving his or her skills over the long term.

Strategies to manage importance

1. Set realistic expectations: Having realistic expectations is crucial to avoid creating excessive importance. Instead of expecting immediate results or guaranteed success, a trader should understand that the process of learning and improving takes time and that losses are a natural part of the journey.

2. Separate ego from results: In trading, ego is often a major source of inner weight. Separating the outcome of a trade from personal self-worth can help maintain a more objective perspective. The success or failure of a trade does not define the trader as a person.

3. Practice Detachment: Practicing detachment from outcomes can be a powerful tool. This doesn't mean being indifferent, but rather accepting the results, whether positive or negative, without significantly affecting the trader's emotional state. This mindset allows for better adaptation and greater resilience to market fluctuations.

Importance is one of the main obstacles that prevent traders from reaching their full potential. Whether it is internal importance, which leads to overvaluation of oneself, or outer weight, which exaggerates the relevance of a trade or event, both generate tensions that negatively affect performance.

Reducing importance does not mean trading without passion or commitment, but rather learning to release unnecessary pressure and accept that losses and mistakes are part of the process. By doing so, the trader can make more objective decisions, learn from each experience, and above all, enjoy the journey without the shackles of perfection and anxiety. As Zeland said, by reducing importance, we come into balance with the world around us and regain the freedom to choose our actions without being slaves to excessive expectations.

Trading is ultimately a continuous learning process. By letting go of over-importance and focusing on progressive improvement, a trader can trade with greater clarity, confidence, and satisfaction. True freedom in trading comes not from controlling every aspect of the market, but from breaking free from emotional shackles and trading from a place of balance and awareness. Reducing importance allows us to access a more effective state of mind, where every decision is made calmly and without the weight of fear or arrogance, leading to a much more successful and sustainable trading practice in the long term.

From struggle to balance

The trading journey can often feel like a constant battle against the market, emotions, and one's own expectations. However, this combative approach brings us face to face with what Vadim Zeland calls "equilibrating forces" or "balancing forces" – those energies that try to restore balance when excessive potential is generated. Instead of fighting these forces, the key is to eliminate the cause of the imbalance: importance.

Importance is the source of most of our trading problems. When we give too much importance to an event, a trade, or our perception of ourselves as traders, we create excessive potential that unleashes forces that act against us. This imbalance manifests as frustration, anxiety, and impulsive decisions that often lead to negative outcomes.

Every time we try to force results in our activity, we are, in effect, building a wall of importance. We may want to overcome a loss quickly, recover capital from a bad trade, or prove our worth with a spectacular success. This wall, built on the foundation of importance, becomes an obstacle of our own making. Rather than trying to climb it or break it with our heads, Zeland suggests a simpler solution: remove a brick from the foundation so that the wall collapses on its own. That brick is the importance we have given to the situation.

When faced with a difficult situation, it is helpful to ask ourselves: Where am I overstepping my boundaries? What am I giving too much importance to? Once we have identified that importance, we must let it go. Fighting is not the solution; the solution is to diminish the importance.

De-emphasizing doesn't mean becoming indifferent or disinterested in trading. Rather, it means approaching the process in a more relaxed and fluid manner, without exaggerating or diminishing the value of our actions or results. If we attribute too much significance to a trade, we increase the tension, which ironically reduces our chances of success.

Imagine you have a trade that you consider key to determining your future as a trader. You have given it so much importance that every small movement in market conditions causes you anxiety, affecting your ability to make rational decisions. This attitude not only creates tension and fear, but also increases the possibility of making mistakes. By diminishing the importance of this specific trade and viewing it as a part of the ongoing learning process, we eliminate excessive potential and allow balance to return.

To stop struggling and start moving towards mental balance, it is essential to develop a philosophical attitude towards trading. It is not about belittling our goals or giving in to circumstances, but about accepting that we cannot always control the market and that each trade is just one more in a long journey.

By reducing the importance of each individual outcome, we eliminate excessive potential and prevent the intervention of equalizing forces. The key is to establish safety mechanisms or "escape routes." These mechanisms help us relax and reduce tension. For example, a trader might make sure that each trade has a defined stop loss to avoid excessive losses. Knowing that risk is controlled, the importance of each trade decreases, allowing for a calmer and more objective attitude.

Another powerful tool for reducing importance is a sense of humor. Being able to laugh at our losses or mistakes, without malice, allows us to release tension and prevent importance from growing. This does not mean that we should take trading lightly, but we should prevent our mistakes from becoming a source of anguish and excessive self-demand.

To apply this concept of balance, every time you prepare to perform a trade, look for any signs of importance that may arise in you. If a trade really has a lot of significance for you, avoid increasing that importance. The best way to do this is to adopt an attitude of improvisation and flexibility. Prepare to perform, but don't over-analyze or exaggerate the preparation, as this will only increase the tension and importance.

The focus should be on the process, not the outcome. If you can divert your attention from the end goal (such as making money) and focus it on the process of executing your strategy in a disciplined manner, the balancing forces will not interfere. This will allow you to operate with greater peace of mind, without the emotional baggage that can lead to impulsive decisions.

Remember that importance seeps into our thoughts similarly to how muscles involuntarily tense when we are stressed. Just as we consciously relax tense muscles, we must learn to relax our minds and let go of the importance we are attributing to each operation. Keeping an "internal watchman" constantly monitoring our emotional state and expectations will help us stay balanced.

It is essential to remember that each individual trade does not determine our overall success as traders. What really matters is the cumulative performance over time. When we reduce the importance of each trade, we can focus on continually improving, rather than treating each outcome as a judgment of our personal worth.

A useful strategy is to focus on improving the process rather than the immediate result. Evaluate your performance based on how you followed your trading plan, not on whether the trade was a winner or a loser. This takes the emotional pressure off and allows you to trade in a more rational manner.

Also, don't forget to diversify your efforts and not put all your expectations on one trade or strategy. If one trade has a bad outcome, it's not the end of the world. Having a diversified focus on different strategies and approaches reduces the importance of each event and helps maintain a more balanced perspective.

One of the most effective ways to move from struggle to balance is through a sense of humor. Laughing at yourself and the mistakes you make in trading, without malice, allows you to release built-up tension and protects you from falling into the trap of self-importance.

A trader who can recognize his mistakes and learn from them without taking himself too seriously is a trader who can stay balanced even in the most challenging situations. Humor is a powerful tool that allows us to accept our humanity, our imperfections, and the fact that we do not always control everything that happens in our environment.

Moving from constant struggle to balance in trading doesn't happen overnight. It requires introspection and constant practice. But by learning to reduce importance, both internal and external, traders can operate more efficiently and calmly, avoiding the emotional sabotage that often accompanies trading activity.

A sense of humor, a relaxed attitude, and the ability to focus on the process rather than the results are key tools to finding mental balance. By stopping fighting our own emotions and market conditions, we can begin to flow with the movements of the environment and achieve our goals in a more harmonious and effective way.

True freedom comes not from controlling every aspect of the market, but from breaking free from emotional shackles and operating from a place of balance. Reducing importance allows us to access a more effective state of mind, where every decision is made calmly and without the weight of fear or arrogance, leading to a much more successful and sustainable trading practice in the long term.

Summary

- Excessive potential arises from giving too much importance to a situation in trading. Keep perspective and avoid exaggerating the significance of a single outcome.
- When there is excess potential, balancing forces act to eliminate it, often causing results opposite to those desired. Avoid obsessing over success or failure.
- Keep an active watch on your emotions. Avoid discontent or frustration, as they put you disadvantaged in trading.
- Replace negative reactions with a positive attitude to operate with greater clarity and prevent balancing forces from acting against you.
- Creating dependency on the outcome of a trade creates excessive potential. Avoid idealizing a strategy or trading opportunity.
- To be successful, operate with detachment, admiring the process without clinging to the outcome.
- The more importance is attributed to a goal, the lower the probability of achieving it. Decreasing the relevance of an operation allows intentions to be fulfilled without blockages.
- Give up feelings of guilt over losses and the need to justify yourself. Learn from mistakes and move on without harsh self-criticism to release the emotional burden.
- See money as a companion attribute, not as the main objective. Accept both gains and losses with serenity.
- By giving up importance, we gain true freedom of choice. To fulfill our desires in trading, it removes excessive relevance from each operation.
- Constant worry creates excessive potential. Take care of your mental and emotional health without obsessing over results, allowing you to operate in a balanced and effective way.

Chapter V

Reactive shift

The topic of "Reactive Shift" addresses a psychological and emotional phenomenon that occurs collectively, where each generation tends to think that the past was better. This concept applies to how traders perceive the financial environment and their performance over time. They often idealize the first moments in which they discovered the financial markets, believing that they were simpler and better times, when, in reality, this perception is influenced by our emotions. This can lead to decisions based on nostalgia, making it difficult to adapt to current conditions. For the trader, learning to identify this tendency is crucial to avoid mistakes that can limit their progress.

Imagine for a moment how you felt when you were first starting out in the world of trading. Everything was exciting, every small triumph felt like a big win, and there was a sense of limitless possibilities. There was a spark of adventure, a constant excitement to learn, and a belief that the financial world was full of opportunities to explore. Every day seemed like a new possibility for growth and success. Over time, it is natural for traders to look back on those initial moments with nostalgia, thinking that conditions were more "favorable."

This is a common trap: the "reactive shift" to an idealized view of the past and the belief that the present is more complicated. This belief can hinder the development of a successful mindset, disconnecting the trader from the present and the current realities of the financial environment. The problem is that this nostalgic thinking can lead the investor to decisions based on emotions and not on current reality, affecting their performance and ability to make effective decisions.

When an investor faces periods of disappointment or loses confidence, he or she may fall into an "reactive shift" to lifelines that he or she perceives as less favorable. This happens because our emotions play a major role in how we interpret our reality. By focusing on the negative, the investor affects his or her decisions and the way he or she perceives the environment. Every negative thought becomes a barrier that prevents him or her from seeing opportunities, even when they are right in front of him or her, reinforcing the perception that "it was better before" and leading to a spiral of self-limitation and frustration. Frustration can make the trader feel that the circumstances are against him or her, which only increases the cycle of negativity and causes more mistakes. This dynamic is especially dangerous because it can become a self-reinforcing cycle: bad results generate negative thoughts, and these negative thoughts lead to worse results.

To better illustrate this concept, let's think of an example from everyday life. Imagine you've started a new job. At first, everything is exciting: the new challenges, the colleagues, the constant learning. Everything seems full of possibilities. But over time, you start to notice the negative aspects: maybe the salary isn't the best, sometimes you have to leave later, pressure, repetitive tasks. Gradually, you focus on the negative and lose motivation. Has the job really changed, or has your perception of it changed? In reality, the job is still the same, but the accumulated negative energy has made you lose sight of what made it interesting.

This is an example of an "reactive shift," where the focus on the negative creates a less favorable version of the same reality. In trading, something similar happens when we hold on to the belief that it was easier or fairer before. The reality is that it has always been complex and has always had its challenges; what changes is how we choose to interpret it and how we adapt. If we allow our perception to be dominated by negativity, we will lose sight of the opportunities that are always present, even in the most difficult times.

One of the keys to avoiding this negative transition is to understand that the financial environment does not deteriorate on its own; what changes is our interpretation of it. The market, as I always say, is a neutral entity: it has no intentions, it does not "turn against you" or conspire to make you lose. It is our attitude and perception that changes, and that is what we must learn to regulate if we want to stay in a state of mind that favors our decisions.

Instead of thinking that conditions have changed for the worse, it is more useful to assume that the environment is constantly changing and that our ability to adapt defines our success or failure. By accepting change as constant, we can learn to flow with the circumstances. Adopting this perspective allows us to see changes as opportunities for learning and improvement, rather than seeing them as obstacles. If the environment changes, we must also change and adapt. The key is to remain flexible and willing to evolve along with the conditions.

Maintaining a mindful attitude is crucial to avoid falling into negative thought cycles. When a trade doesn't go as you expected, it's easy to fall into the trap of thinking that everything is no longer the same or that conditions have become insurmountable. But what if, instead of focusing on the loss, you decided to see it as an opportunity to learn something new about the market or even yourself? Every mistake or obstacle can be a valuable lesson.

By adopting this perspective, every loss becomes an opportunity to improve and adjust your approach. It's not about ignoring losses, but rather seeing them as an inevitable and beneficial component of the learning process. From every failed trade, a lesson can be learned that, if applied correctly, can make a significant difference in the future. The real difference between a successful trader and an unsuccessful one lies in the latter's ability to learn from their mistakes without allowing them to define them.

Trading is not just about analyzing charts and applying strategies; it is also about understanding how your emotions influence your decisions. Accepting that the environment is constantly changing and that what worked in the past may not work in the present is part of growing as an investor. The ability to detach from the past and focus on the present is critical to long-term success. To overcome the "reactive shift," it is necessary to work on your mindset.

Techniques such as mindfulness can be very useful, as they help you stay focused on the present and accept things as they are, without judging them or comparing them to the past. Practicing mindfulness allows you to observe your thoughts and emotions without becoming attached to them, which is essential to prevent negative thought patterns from taking hold and affecting your behavior as a trader. Being present in each moment and acting from full awareness can make the difference between reacting emotionally and responding rationally and effectively.

Additionally, it is important to surround yourself with tools and habits that promote an objective view of the market. Keeping a trading journal not only allows you to keep track of your trades, but also of your emotions and thoughts at every moment. This will help you identify negative patterns and correct them before they become an obstacle to your progress. A trading journal allows you to reflect on your decisions, understand why you took certain actions, and how to improve in the future. It is also useful to have an analysis routine that allows you to dispassionately review what has happened, focusing on facts and not subjective interpretations. This routine can include a weekly or monthly review of your trades, where you can identify patterns and adjust your strategies according to what you have learned. Regularly reflecting on your trades will help you maintain a mindset focused on continuous learning, which is key to long-term growth.

This chapter could add a lot of value to your career if approached correctly. We could focus on how to avoid falling into negative thought cycles after a bad trade and how to regain confidence and clarity. For example, we could highlight the importance of having a clear system of rules that maintains objectivity and discipline, even when emotions threaten to get out of control.

A well-defined system not only provides structure for decision-making, but also reduces the influence of emotions in times of uncertainty. Having clear and defined rules eliminates ambiguity at critical moments and allows you to act with greater confidence and security. The market will always offer opportunities, but only those who stay in the right frame of mind will be able to take advantage of them. Having a clear structure and sticking to it can be the difference between acting on impulse and making informed decisions.

Remember, the market is neither your enemy nor your friend; it simply is. You decide how to interact with it. If you can avoid the trap of romanticizing the past and maintain an open and positive attitude towards the present, you will be one step closer to achieving your goals as a trader. "reactive shift" is not inevitable; it is simply a sign that you need to readjust your approach and refocus on what really matters: your growth and evolution as a trader. Every moment focused on the past is a lost moment to act in the present and build a better future.

The key is to embrace change, learn from every experience, and maintain a growth mindset. If you manage to do this, you will not only be a better trader, but also a more resilient and adaptable person, capable of facing any challenge that life or the financial environment puts in your path.

Every experience in the market, whether good or bad, is an opportunity to grow and improve. By adopting this mindset, you not only develop your technical skills, but you also strengthen your character and resilience, essential characteristics for long-term success in the world of trading.

Loop of Influence

The concept of the "Loop of Influence" refers to how pendulums, external forces that manipulate our emotions, drag us into a spiral of negativity. In the context of trading, the loop of Influence manifests when traders get caught up in the negative narrative of the financial environment.

This phenomenon can lead traders to focus disproportionately on negative news, losses, and fear, while positive opportunities go unnoticed. It is a self-defeating cycle in which negative thoughts generate more negative thoughts, and the trader sinks deeper into the "funnel."

Human nature has a tendency to react more intensely to negative events, something that goes back to our primitive survival instincts. This inclination makes sense from an evolutionary perspective, as our ancestors needed to pay more attention to threats to ensure their survival. On the other hand, in the context of trading, this tendency works against us. Traders tend to react more strongly to news of losses, declines in financial conditions, or negative predictions, which capture their attention much more powerfully than positive news or market advances.

This creates a situation where traders feel trapped in a constant cycle of worry, fear, and stress, leading them to make irrational decisions. The loop of Influence begins when the trader allows these emotions to control their decisions, thus increasing the likelihood of making mistakes and perpetuating the cycle of negativity.

An investor may become aware of a negative news story affecting the financial environment, such as a drastic decline in indices due to a political or economic circumstance. This news becomes the first "push" of the pendulum. If the investor reacts with fear or anxiety, he or she will begin to focus on that narrative, seeking out more negative information, discussing it with others, and reinforcing the idea that conditions are against him or her.

This focus not only consumes his or her time and energy, but also prevents him or her from seeing the bigger picture and the opportunities that might be emerging. Each time the trader reinforces this narrative, the pendulum swing intensifies, causing his or her mind to become more and more attuned to the frequency of that fear and negative narrative.

Geopolitical events and wars are powerful examples of how external factors can trigger this loop of Influence. When armed conflicts, political crises, or international tensions occur, the constant stream of negative news tends to capture traders' attention disproportionately. These events generate fear and uncertainty in the financial realm, leading many investors to act impulsively and erratically. Media coverage of these events is often intensely negative and alarmist, further exacerbating traders' anxiety, making them feel they must react quickly to protect their capital. As a result, investors are drawn into a cycle of fear and reactivity, making decisions based on panic rather than objective and rational analysis.

In an international conflict, the news is often filled with information highlighting instability and danger. Traders following this news may be overwhelmed by the feeling that the environment will become increasingly chaotic, and they start making hasty decisions to avoid further losses. This attitude often leads them to sell assets at the worst possible moment, only to see conditions recover after a while, which fuels their frustration and further reinforces the loop of Influence. Such behavior is based on emotional reaction, not on careful analysis of the possibilities and risks, which is the real problem behind the negative spiral.

The main problem is that as the trader focuses more on this negative news, his perception of the financial environment becomes distorted. Fear and anxiety start to color his entire vision, causing him to search and find only evidence that confirms his emotional state. He ignores any signal that might indicate a positive opportunity. He might miss a clear technical pattern that indicates a good entry, simply because his mind is completely absorbed by the fear that conditions will get even worse. This attitude turns the trader into a victim of the pendulum, caught in the funnel and dragged towards lifelines, where fear and hopelessness become his predominant reality.

To avoid falling into this loop of Influence, it is essential for the trader to maintain a balanced perspective and avoid feeding the collective force with his or her own energy. This means learning to recognize when one is reacting emotionally and taking a pause before acting. Discipline is key: establishing clear rules that limit the influence of emotions in decision-making can help prevent the trader from falling victim to this negative cycle. Measuring emotional response is a powerful tool; if you feel that a news story is affecting you too much, you might choose to step away from the screens, take a deep breath, and calmly reevaluate your strategy before making impulsive decisions. This type of pause can be the difference between reacting hastily and responding rationally.

Furthermore, it is important for traders to be aware of the nature of news and how it is presented. Often, headlines and coverage of geopolitical events are designed to grab attention, exaggerating the drama of the situation and provoking intense emotional responses. The media has an interest in attracting audiences, and that often means presenting situations in the most alarming light possible. Investors must learn to filter information, distinguish between noise and relevant facts, and avoid being swept up in widespread panic. This requires a critical mindset and the ability to challenge the prevailing narrative.

Developing a routine that includes objective analysis and limiting exposure to sensational media can be key to maintaining objectivity and avoiding getting caught in the loop of Influence. For example, traders can set specific times to check the news and focus the rest of the time on technical and fundamental analysis. It is also helpful to have reliable and objective sources of information, rather than relying solely on large media networks that tend to dramatize events. Keeping a trading journal that records not only trades, but also thoughts and emotions during trades, can help identify patterns of emotional reaction and correct them over time.

Another technique that can be very helpful is the practice of mindfulness. By learning to be present and aware of the current moment, traders can reduce the impact of negative emotions and avoid being swept away by the collective force. Meditation and other mindfulness practices can help traders observe their thoughts without reacting to them, which is crucial to staying calm and clear in high volatility situations. By being fully aware of their emotions and how they affect their decisions, a trader can act from a place of serenity and objectivity, rather than being pushed by fear or the euphoria of the moment.

Ultimately, avoiding the loop of Influence is about developing a resilient and disciplined mindset. It is about recognizing that while external events such as wars and political crises can have a significant impact, the real power lies in how we react to them. Traders who manage to maintain a balanced perspective, who properly filter information, and who avoid feeding the fear cycle are those who can navigate even the most turbulent situations successfully. The key is to understand that the financial environment is neutral; it is our interpretation and our response that defines whether we become victims of the pendulum or conscious and successful investors.

Summary

- The "Poop of Influence" describes how traders get caught up in the negative market narrative, focusing on news and losses instead of seeing opportunities.

- Geopolitical events and wars can act as triggers that drag investors into the fear narrative, generating impulsive and harmful decisions.

- The concept of "Catastrophe" explains how constant exposure to negative information can lead traders to become victims of their own emotions, affecting their results.

- Filtering the information we receive and avoiding overexposure to alarmist news is key to maintaining objectivity in trading.

- Practicing neutrality, avoiding impulsive reactions and contributing positive content are effective strategies to avoid falling into the funnel of conflict.

Chapter VI

Stream of variants

The "Stream of Variants" is a key concept developed by Vadim Zeland in his Transurfing model. This concept describes a universal information field that we all have access to and that contains all possible events, scenarios and discoveries that can manifest in our reality. In Zeland's thinking, this field represents the "energy matrix" or pattern of what can happen and how it unfolds, thus providing an inexhaustible source of inspiration, knowledge and insight. The idea behind this concept is that everything that exists, has existed or can exist is available as information in this stream, and it is our ability to tune into it that allows us to access new ideas and visions. It is an approach that redefines our understanding of creativity, knowledge and connection to the universe.

According to Zeland, the field of options is a place where information exists in potential form before it materializes into our reality. The conscious mind does not have the direct ability to read this information, but the subconscious can connect with it. It is through this connection that our feelings, intuitions, creative ideas, and discoveries arise. First, the information reaches the subconscious, and then the conscious mind interprets it and transforms it into words, symbols, music, art, and more.

This stream of variants is, according to Zeland, a gift to the mind, although humans do not always realize it. This source of inspiration, which is often ignored or misinterpreted, is actually direct access to universal wisdom that goes beyond what the intellect can achieve on its own.

To illustrate, we can think of how certain scientific discoveries or artistic advances have not necessarily been the product of step-by-step logical analysis, but often seem to have come "out of nowhere." Great inventions and masterpieces have been inspired by sudden flashes of insight, as if the information had come from a deeper place.

This place, according to Zeland, is the stream of variants, and the subconscious is the channel that connects us to it. History is full of examples of scientists and artists who have had seemingly spontaneous flashes of genius, as if the solution to a problem or the inspiration for a work had been "downloaded" from an unknown source. These moments of clarity, where the solution or inspiration seems to come effortlessly, are precisely manifestations of the stream of variants.

In this sense, the conscious mind functions as an "interpreter" of the data coming from the subconscious, organizing and shaping it in the material world. However, the mind alone cannot create something entirely new from the unknown. True creativity and inspiration come from connecting to this universal information field, which provides us with a broader perspective outside the boundaries of strict logic. This connection allows us to access a level of knowledge and creativity that is not restricted by the usual limitations of rational thought. Instead of creating from scratch, we tune into an infinite source of information and give it a tangible form through our conscious mind and our abilities.

By contextualizing the "Stream of Variations" in trading, we can see how this concept can help traders better understand the importance of intuition and connecting with their subconscious. Instead of relying solely on technical analysis and objective data, traders could benefit from paying attention to their gut feelings and intuitive feelings, which are one way to access this stream of information. Intuition is not simply a random feeling; it is the subconscious connecting with the field of variations and providing information that can be useful in making decisions. Traders who develop the ability to listen to and trust their intuition are tapping into a source of information that goes beyond charts and numbers, and that can give them a significant advantage.

A trader might get an unexplainable feeling about a trade, whether it's a positive signal to enter the market or a warning that something could go wrong. These feelings can't always be backed up by hard data, but they often turn out to be accurate. This is because the subconscious has access to broader and more in-depth information, and can detect patterns and risks that the conscious mind might miss. The subconscious is constantly processing information at a level that isn't always accessible to the conscious mind, and can identify subtle signals that could be indicators of a change in the financial environment. Relying on these feelings can make the difference between a successful trade and an avoided loss.

Learning to go with the flow of the variations means ceasing to resist the information that comes from within us and beginning to trust more in our hunches and flashes of intuition. This does not mean abandoning analysis and trading exclusively based on intuition, but rather integrating both: conscious analysis and intuitive flashes. In this way, the trader can develop a more balanced and broader perspective, taking advantage not only of objective data, but also of the information that comes from the flow of the variations. It is the integration of reason and intuition that allows one to trade in a more complete way, making decisions that are based on both rational analysis and a deeper, more intuitive perception of what is happening.

Going with the flow also means letting go of fighting market conditions. Many traders get frustrated when the environment doesn't behave the way they had anticipated, and this frustration can lead to impulsive decisions. Instead of fighting the direction circumstances are taking, going with the flow means accepting what is happening and adapting. By doing so, a trader can avoid decisions motivated by ego or fear, and align themselves with the natural flow of information and trends.

Going with the flow means recognizing that the financial environment has its own pace and direction, and that our job is not to force an outcome, but to adapt and find the best way to navigate those waters. Traders who manage to align themselves with the flow are often those who find opportunities even in times of high volatility, as they don't resist, but rather adapt.

Another important aspect of the flow of variants in the context of trading is the ability to recognize when not to act. Sometimes the best decision is to take no action at all, and this can also be guided by intuition.

The flow of variants can provide signals not only to enter a trade, but also to know when it is best to stay on the sidelines and wait. This patience and ability to listen to intuition is critical to avoid trading impulsively and making mistakes that could have been avoided. Going with the flow means knowing when to act and when to wait, and this wisdom can only come from a deep connection with our subconscious.

In short, the "Flow of Variations" is a powerful source of information and inspiration that we can all learn to harness. In the context of trading, it involves trusting intuition, flowing with the conditions, and no longer resisting what happens. By integrating this approach with rational analysis, traders can make better decisions and operate in a more fluid and connected manner with the financial environment. This integration of the rational and the intuitive allows investors to be more adaptable and creative, and to face challenges with an open and flexible mindset. Flowing with the flow of variations is ultimately a way of trading that is aligned with the natural forces of the market, which can provide a significant advantage in such a competitive and changing environment.

Connecting with the field of variants

The concept of "Knowledge from Nowhere" is another fundamental element developed by Vadim Zeland in his Transurfing model. This concept refers to the ability of certain people to access information or ideas that do not seem to come from any logical or rational source, but rather arise from a deeper and more inexplicable place. Zeland explains that these insights come from the universal information field, also known as the space of variants. Although we all have access to this field, only a select little manage to perceive these data clearly. For most people, these insights appear as hunches, intuitions or vague ideas, which seem to arise without an obvious cause.

In Zeland's model, the subconscious can connect with this information space, while the conscious mind, being always busy with internal monologue and logical reasoning, has difficulty listening to and understanding the signals coming from the subconscious. This disconnection is the reason why we often fail to take advantage of the potential of these intuitions or creative ideas. The mind focuses on what it already knows, classifying information into established categories and trying to put a label on everything it perceives. By "categories" I mean the mental structures we use to group concepts and simplify our understanding of the world. For example, when we think of a category like "fruit," we immediately think of items like apples, oranges, or bananas because our mind groups these items under one label. Similarly, we classify ideas and experiences with labels to understand them quickly.

However, when something comes along that doesn't fit into any of the established categories, such as a wholly new concept or experience, our minds tend to reject it or have difficulty processing it. When information comes along that doesn't fit into these categories, our minds perceive it as incomprehensible, which makes it difficult to use. This limitation can prevent us from accessing valuable knowledge that could transform our lives if we recognized and used it.

This process manifests itself in science and art. Many scientists and artists have described their moments of inspiration as coming suddenly, almost as if the answer emerged from a mysterious source. Rather than being the result of prolonged logical analysis, the solution or inspiration appears spontaneously, like a flash of insight. According to Zeland, this flash is the connection of the subconscious to an unrealized sector of the space of variants, where information exists in its purest form, without interpretations or labels. In other words, creativity is not just a matter of rational thought, but an act of connecting to a deeper, unknown source.

To illustrate this concept, we can refer to the story of the scientist Friedrich August Kekulé, who discovered the structure of benzene thanks to a dream. Kekulé had been working for a long time on the problem of determining the structure of this molecule, but could not find a logical solution.

One night, while resting, Kekulé dreamed of a snake biting its tail, forming a circle. Upon awakening, he had a revelation: the structure of benzene was cyclic, something he had not considered until then. This image, seemingly emerging from nowhere, allowed him to formulate one of the most important theories of organic chemistry. This example shows how the subconscious, by connecting with the field of variants, can bring information that is not available to the conscious mind through rational thought. In the same way, artists such as Salvador Dalí and writers such as Mary Shelley also recounted how their works emerged from visions or dreams, illustrating the idea that genuine creativity is fueled by something beyond conventional reasoning.

The main challenge in harnessing this knowledge that comes "from nowhere" lies in learning to synchronize the mind and soul. The mind, which represents our conscious and rational part, needs to learn to listen to the signals of the soul, which is where the subconscious resides and the ability to connect with universal information. To complete this, it is necessary to learn to reduce mental noise and allow the soul's signals to reach consciousness. This synchronization process is not easy, but it is essential if we wish to access a deeper level of understanding and take advantage of the wisdom that is already available to us.

An effective technique for achieving this synchronization is meditation. By meditating, we can quiet the mind's constant internal monologue and create a space of silence where signals from the subconscious can be heard. It is in these moments of calm and stillness that feelings, intuitions, or flashes of inspiration are most likely to arise.

Meditation not only helps reduce mental noise, but also improves our ability to focus and pay attention to internal sensations, which is essential for picking up on signals from the soul. Regular meditation practice helps us establish a more open channel between the conscious mind and the subconscious, allowing information to flow more naturally and effectively.

Another way to develop this connection is to pay attention to feelings of inner comfort or discomfort. The soul communicates through sensations; for example, when something seems "right" or "wrong" to us for no apparent reason. Learning to recognize these sensations and give them importance can help us make decisions that are more aligned with our intuition and our true self. Many times, the mind tends to ignore these sensations because they cannot be explained logically, but if we manage to pay attention to them, we can access a deeper and wiser level of knowledge. This involves cultivating the ability to discern between mental noise and authentic signals from the soul, which can transform our way of making decisions.

An everyday example might be making important decisions. Let's say a person is considering changing jobs. The conscious mind might analyze all the variables—salary, benefits, stability, etc.—and come to a conclusion based on that objective data. However, the soul might be sending a signal of discomfort, a feeling that something is not right, even though all the logical data points to it being a good decision. If the person learns to listen to that inner voice, he or she might be able to avoid deciding that, while rationally correct, might not be the most appropriate for his or her well-being and personal fulfillment. These types of decisions are the ones that, when intuition is considered, can lead to results that better align us with our life purpose and happiness.

In the realm of creativity, learning to listen to the voice of the soul can be the key to accessing genuine inspiration. Artists who manage to create masterpieces do so not only through technical mastery, but also because they can connect with something deeper and let inspiration flow through them. This inspiration does not come from the rational mind, but from the soul, which is connected to the field of variants. Practicing activities that encourage relaxation and a state of flow, such as walking in nature, listening to music, or simply disconnecting from daily worries, can help open this connection and allow ideas to flow more easily. This state of flow, also known as "flow," is a state in which the mind and body work in perfect synchrony, and time seems to stop, allowing creativity to express itself unhindered.

In addition to meditation and flow state, another useful tool to strengthen the connection with the subconscious is creative visualization. Visualizing our goals or situations in a relaxed manner, without forcing outcomes, can help the subconscious to tune into the sectors of the field of options that contain the reality we wish to experience. This visualization exercise not only focuses us, but also allows the soul to connect with the favorable variants, providing a sense of clarity and direction that goes beyond logical reasoning.

In short, the "Knowledge from Nowhere" are a manifestation of our ability to connect with a universal field of information through the subconscious. To take advantage of this ability, it is essential to learn to synchronize the mind and soul, quieting the mental noise and paying attention to internal sensations and feelings.

Meditating, practicing mindfulness, fostering the flow state and learning to listen to our inner voice are powerful tools to access these insights that can transform our creativity, our decisions and our life in general. By opening ourselves to this deeper source of information, we can discover new possibilities, innovate in unexpected ways and live in a way that is more aligned with our authentic self. The key is to trust that inner voice that guides us and allow the wisdom of the soul to influence our decisions and actions, thus transforming our world in a meaningful and enriching way.

Pleader, Bitter, and Fighter

Zeland presents us with three archetypes of behavior in the face of life's challenges and circumstances: the pleader, the bitter, and the fighter. Each of these roles describes a specific attitude that human beings tend to adopt when faced with difficult situations or when seeking to achieve their goals.

Despite this, none of these approaches is ideal from a Transurfing perspective, as each involves a form of pendulum dependency and a lack of fluidity in aligning with the space of variants. Understanding the nature of these roles and their limitations allows us to consciously choose a different path, one in which we can be masters of our destiny and act in a way that is aligned with our true intentions.

The pleader is someone who gives in to life and passively accepts whatever fate has in store for them. They take no responsibility for their own existence and just drift along like a paper boat. By taking this stance, the pleader becomes a puppet, letting the pendulums take control of their life. Instead of deciding for themselves, the pleader resigns, complains, and asks higher powers to grant them what they want. But life does not respond to passive supplication, as this approach lacks the strength to create real change.

This attitude creates a disconnection with personal power and perpetuates the feeling of helplessness. An everyday example of the pleader could be a person who, dissatisfied with their job, takes no action to look for something better and instead constantly complains, hoping that life or someone else will fix it. This person finds themselves trapped in a cycle of waiting and frustration, not understanding that they have the power to change their situation if they choose to act.

On the other hand, the bitter is someone who is not satisfied with what life offers him, but instead of taking effective action, he adopts an attitude of constant complaint and demands what he believes is his due. This attitude only generates resistance and reinforces the potentials of importance, which end up working against him. The bitter not only complains, but also blames others for his problems and considers that the world is indebted to him. This way of thinking reinforces the role of victim and feeds negativity, creating a vicious circle where discontent attracts more situations that justify that discontent.

An example of the bitter could be a person who, upon not getting a promotion at work, blames his colleagues and bosses, and remains trapped in bitterness and anger, without realizing that this attitude distances him even further from his goals. Instead of looking for a solution or strengthening his skills, the bitter focuses on blaming and complaining, which only perpetuates his dissatisfaction.

Finally, there is the fighter, who decides to take charge of his or her life, but does so through constant struggle. The fighter believes that to achieve his or her goals he or she must fight against all odds, elbow his or her way through, and compete with others. Although this attitude is more productive than that of the pleader or the bitter, it is still far from the approach proposed by Transurfing, as it involves a constant drain of energy and a perception of life as a battle.

The fighter can achieve his or her goals, but always at a high cost, and in the end, the sense of accomplishment is overshadowed by exhaustion and sacrifice. This approach promotes the idea that nothing valuable is obtained without suffering, which limits our ability to experience the process with joy.

An example of the fighter could be someone who works tirelessly to build a successful career, sacrificing his or her health and personal relationships in the process, believing that this is the only way to succeed. Even if he or she achieves professional success, the lack of balance leaves him or her with a feeling of emptiness and an emotional cost that overshadows the achievement.

Vadim Zeland suggests an alternative approach to these three archetypes, an attitude we might call that of the Master of Destiny. Instead of asking like the pleader, demanding like the bitter, or fighting like the fighter, the Master of Destiny simply "goes and takes" what he or she wants. This does not mean acting arrogantly or disrespectfully toward others, but rather adopting an attitude of confidence and determination, not giving undue importance to obstacles or creating potentials for conflict. The Master of

Destiny does not see challenges as insurmountable barriers, but as opportunities to learn and grow. By letting go of importance and going with the flow of the variations, opportunities open up that seem to come effortlessly because one is aligned with the reality one wishes to create. This attitude is based on the premise that we all have the power to generate our circumstances and that we do not need to fight the world to get what we want.

To illustrate this approach, imagine someone who wants to start his own business. Instead of waiting for a "sign" from the universe, like the pleader, or complaining about the lack of financial support, like the bitter, or working tirelessly, sacrificing everything, like the fighter, the Master of

Destiny decides to act consciously. He defines his goal clearly, begins to take concrete steps, seeks resources and contacts, but without giving in to despair or creating resistance. He maintains the confidence that if he is aligned with his purpose, things will happen naturally. In this way, he flows with the flow of the variants, moving towards his goal without forcing things, but also without remaining passive. This attitude not only allows him to advance towards his goal, but also to enjoy the process, finding balance and satisfaction along the way. The key is to act with intention and without the burden of excessive importance that creates tension and resistance.

The key is to let go of importance. Importance creates tension, resistance, and loss of energy. When we stop attributing excessive importance to obstacles, they begin to fade away on their own. Importance, both external and internal, acts as an anchor that keeps us tied to difficult situations and negative thought patterns. In this way, the Master of his

Destiny does not see life as a struggle, but as a game in which he can freely choose and move the pieces with confidence and serenity. By adopting this attitude, he becomes the true creator of his reality, able to achieve his goals without the unnecessary burdens of conflict, resignation, or discontent.

Instead of fighting against circumstances, he learns to navigate between them, taking advantage of the favorable currents of the space of variants. The feeling of fluidity and ease that is experienced when acting without the burden of importance is what allows the results to arrive more effectively and with less emotional wear and tear.

The invitation of this chapter is to reflect on which of these roles we are assuming in our lives, and to consider the possibility of becoming Masters of our Destiny. Instead of letting the pendulums drive us or fighting against them, we can choose to align ourselves with the flow of the space of variants and simply take what is already available to us. True freedom lies in this ability to choose our own path without the weight of importance, flowing confidently towards what we desire. By becoming Masters of our Destiny, we begin to experience a reality more aligned with our desires and purposes, a reality in which we do not need to fight against the current or resign ourselves to whatever comes our way.

We can live with intention, enjoying the process and knowing that we are on the right path. This attitude allows us to be more aware of our choices, take responsibility for our actions, and live with a sense of freedom and purpose that transcends the limitations of the previous archetypes. It is an invitation to live with plenitude, confidence and authenticity, taking control of our lives without unnecessary resistance and with the certainty that everything we need is already within our reach, waiting to be taken.

An alternative to the Fighter

We will consider a third alternative to the extremes of the pleader, the bitter, and the Fighter: learning to move intentionally with the flow of life. Unlike the pleader, who goes with no will, or the fighter, who fights relentlessly against the current, this approach seeks to harness the natural flow of the variants to achieve our goals in a more fluid and effective way. The key is to find the balance between acting with intention and not creating unnecessary resistance, allowing ourselves to be guided in the most favorable direction.

Zeland explains that the flow of variants is like a natural flow of events and circumstances that are already organized in the space of variants. It is like a naturally flowing river that, if we know how to navigate, can take us where we want to go without having to frantically row against the current or let ourselves be carried away without control. The current contains the optimal solutions to our problems and, by learning to flow with it, we can find those paths that require less energy and effort. Learning to go with the flow does not mean being passive, but rather adopting an attitude of full awareness that allows us to take advantage of what life offers us efficiently

In everyday life, this means not overcomplicating things and continually looking for the simplest solution. Let's say we need to find a place to buy a gift for our child for Christmas. Instead of overanalyzing the situation and running halfway around town following a complex plan, we could trust our instincts and start with the shops nearby. Often, what we need is closer than we think, but the mind, under the pressure of importance, tends to look for complicated solutions.

This not only creates stress, but it also deviates us from the most direct and efficient solution. Learning to trust simplicity allows us to free ourselves from the burden of excessive worry. Another example would be someone who has a long to-do list. Instead of stressing over which one is the most important and trying to plan every detail, they can simply start with the task that is closest at hand and can be done easily. This way, the natural flow of actions will guide them to complete the rest without so much stress and wear and tear. Acting in a simple and direct manner makes everything fit together naturally, without the need to create artificial problems.

In the context of trading, going with the flow involves learning to recognize trends without trying to anticipate or force a trade. Many traders, adopting the role of the fighter, attempt to fight against the conditions, believing that with enough effort and analysis they can overcome them. But the financial environment is a force that cannot be controlled, and this constant struggle leads to exhaustion and often losses.

The fighter mindset in trading, while courageous, often results in failed attempts to get ahead of market movements, which can lead to frustration and emotional burnout. In contrast, a trader who goes with the flow learns to observe objectively, without attachment or excessive importance, and make decisions that align with the prevailing trends. If a clear uptrend presents itself, the trader who goes with the flow will take advantage of that direction rather than trying to predict the exact moment when it will change course.

By reducing importance and accepting the natural flow of circumstances, less potential for conflict is created and decisions are made with more clarity and less tension. This attitude also allows the trader to be more flexible and adapt better to changes, as he does not feel obliged to constantly fight against the direction of the market.

For example, imagine an investor who is watching a bullish trend in Bitcoin. The fighter might try to find the exact point where the trend will change, looking to enter a short trade in hopes of capturing maximum profit.

However, this approach often leads to frustration, as it is very difficult to accurately predict that change. Instead of fighting the trend, a trader who goes with the flow might simply wait for a confirmation that the trend is continuing and enter a long position to take advantage of the move that is already occurring. This approach not only reduces risk, but also allows for trading with greater peace of mind and confidence, taking advantage of the natural flow instead of resisting it. In this way, the investor achieves more consistent results and feels less emotionally drained, as he is not trying to beat the market, but rather flow with it.

The key to moving with the flow is to let go of importance. Importance, both internal and external, is what creates tension and resistance, which in turn creates excessive potentials that distort our perception and hinder our actions. When we stop attributing excessive importance to outcomes or obstacles, we begin to see the clearer, simpler path.

This might mean stopping obsessing over every move and instead trusting strategy and allowing trades to unfold without constant intervention. Just like in life, when we go with the flow, we can find optimal opportunities without as much effort or wear and tear. This doesn't mean acting without strategy, but rather trusting that our preparation and knowledge will allow us to make the best decisions without forcing the process. The ability to let go of unnecessary control and let things unfold at their own pace is critical to reducing stress and improving results in both trading and other areas of life.

Let's also imagine someone who wants to improve their physical health. The fighter approach would be to throw themselves into an extremely intense workout routine, believing that only through suffering and sacrifice will they be able to achieve their goals. This approach can lead to burnout, injury, and even early quitting due to pressure and burnout. Instead, going with the flow would involve finding a physical activity that you enjoy and can do consistently, without exhausting yourself or pushing yourself.

You might start with daily walks or dance classes, allowing your body to get used to the movement and enjoying the process. Over time, you could increase the intensity of the exercises naturally, without feeling like you're fighting against yourself. In this way, achieving your goals becomes a much more bearable and sustainable process. Also, by enjoying the activity, motivation stays high and results come more smoothly, without the feeling of constantly fighting your body or circumstances.

Vadim Zeland reminds us that the stream of variants already contains within itself the optimal solutions to our problems. Often, the mind, under the influence of pendulums and importance, is bent on finding complicated solutions to simple problems. The stream of variants offers us an easier alternative: trusting the natural flow of events and acting with smooth, conscious movements. This does not mean being passive, but learning to act harmonizing with circumstances, without creating unnecessary tension.

Letting go of resistance allows us to take advantage of opportunities that present themselves more effectively, without wasting energy on useless struggles. By adopting this approach, we can discover that many of the obstacles we perceived were actually created by our own mind, and that the true solution was always there, waiting to be taken without complications.

We have to learn to let go, to let go of the need to control every detail, and to trust that the natural flow of life will take us where we need to be, as long as we maintain a mindful attitude and are willing to adjust the rudder when necessary. Instead of fighting against the current or drifting aimlessly, we can be like a skilled navigator who knows the power of the river and knows how to use it to his advantage. By moving with the flow, we reduce wear and tear, make more effective decisions, and align ourselves with the optimal solutions already available in the space of variants.

This attitude not only allows us to achieve our goals more efficiently, but it also helps us enjoy the process more, be at peace with ourselves, and experience a life with less stress and more satisfaction. The current of life is always there, ready to guide us; we just need to learn to trust it and let it carry us toward our goals naturally.

How to read the signs?

Vadim Zeland introduces the concept of "guiding signs" to navigate the stream of variants more effectively. These signs are manifestations that the world constantly presents to us and that, if we know how to interpret them correctly, can help us avoid obstacles or take advantage of opportunities along the way. Life speaks to us in many ways, and it is essential to learn to listen to and understand these messages that often manifest themselves as small coincidences, intuitions or even seemingly random events.

Guiding signals function as indicators of possible turns in the stream of variants, pointing out significant changes that may be occurring or about to occur. These signals can take many forms, from situations that catch our attention unexpectedly to phrases that someone says to us spontaneously.

The key is to recognize when something is out of the ordinary, when there appears to be a qualitative difference in what is happening. That difference can indicate a transition to another lifeline that could be more favorable or less favorable, depending on how we respond.

Imagine that you were leaving home rushing for an important meeting, but then you realize that you forgot something and you have to go back. For many people, this could be interpreted as a negative sign, a bad omen. If, upon returning, you start to feel uneasy or worried that "going back brings bad luck," this attitude can affect you negatively and move you to a less favorable life path, where obstacles continue to appear. However, if you take this incident calmly, simply as a reminder that something was forgotten and without attributing a negative emotional charge to it, you could prevent this disturbance from affecting the rest of your day.

In the context of trading, guiding signals can be crucial to making smart decisions and avoiding unnecessary risks. Experienced traders know that sometimes the financial environment gives off "signals" that indicate a possible trend change. These signals can be specific patterns on charts, unexpected news, or even an intuitive feeling that something is not right. A trader who agrees with these signals will be able to adjust their positions and minimize the risk of losses. Conversely, ignoring these warnings can lead to impulsive and costly decisions.

Consider the example of an investor who, while monitoring the market, notices unusual volatility in the price of an asset he has been thinking of entering. Instead of jumping in immediately and riding the general euphoria, he decides to pause and pay attention to the signals: he sees an increase in sales volume and some news that could indicate a drastic change in market sentiment. Interpreting these signals as a warning, the trader decides to wait before entering, thus avoiding a potential drop that others, less attentive, did not anticipate.

It's important to note that signs are not always clear-cut, nor should they be interpreted literally or superstitiously. Signs are simply indications that something is changing. For example, if you're driving and suddenly encounter a series of small obstacles, such as red lights or a line of cars that slows you down, this could be a signal for you to slow down, not just in a physical sense, but also in a mental sense: an invitation to reconsider your approach or reflect on your haste. It could be a warning to avoid a risky situation later on.

The greatest challenge with guiding signs is learning to differentiate between what is actually a sign and what is simply a random event with no further meaning. Not everything that happens is a sign from the universe; in fact, most things are not. This is why Zeland suggests that we should pay attention to those situations that somehow give us a different impression, as if something in our environment has changed in quality. It is also crucial to avoid creating excessive potentials by worrying too much about every little event, as this could lead us to see signs where there are none, thus falling into paranoia or superstition.

For those looking to move more efficiently with the flow of life, recognizing guiding signs can be a powerful tool. The key is to maintain an aware, calm, and open attitude, but without becoming obsessed. If a sign catches your attention and gives you a negative or alert feeling, you can consider it a warning to adjust your course or take additional precautions. On the other hand, if the sign gives you a calm or positive feeling, it could be confirmation that you are headed in the right direction.

In short, guiding signs are a way for the flow of variants to point out possible changes that are coming. We need to be alert, but not obsessed, with those little messages that can help us adjust our course to move more fluidly and effectively. Life is always speaking to us, and learning to listen to it can make a huge difference in how we navigate our circumstances and achieve our goals.

The importance of guiding signs lies in their ability to provide us with information about what might be going on around us, even when we can't see it clearly. By learning to recognize these signs, we can act in a more informed and proactive manner, avoiding impulsive decisions that could lead us astray from our goals.

Let's say you're in the middle of an important project and everything seems to be going well, but one day you encounter a series of small setbacks: an email that gets lost, a client who cancels a meeting, or a crash on your computer. Instead of getting frustrated and trying to force things back to normal, you could interpret these obstacles as a sign that something needs adjusting, whether it's in your approach, the way you're managing the project, or even your expectations. Taking a moment to reflect and readjust could prevent a small complication from turning into a big problem later on.

Additionally, guiding signs can also appear in the form of opportunities that we don't initially recognize as such. Often, we are so focused on a specific goal that we ignore other possibilities that might be even better. For example, imagine that you are looking for a job in a particular sector, but during your search an offer comes to you in a different area. If you are very closed to new opportunities, you might dismiss this offer without thinking about it. However, if you consider the possibility that this offer is a sign that the universe is presenting to you, you might discover that it is an opportunity even more aligned with your talents and aspirations. This type of openness to signs is what allows us to move with greater flexibility and better adapt to changes.

In the trading arena, this also applies. A trader who becomes too attached to a specific analysis may miss important signals that the financial environment is offering. He may be waiting for a technical pattern to confirm an entry, but the environment is showing signs of weakness that doesn't fit with his initial analysis. If the trader is too attached to a single strategy, he may ignore these signals and enter a bad trade. However, if he is open to the possibility that conditions are indicating something different, he will be able to adjust his strategy and avoid losses. This flexible and attentive approach allows him to not only minimize risks, but also to take better advantage of opportunities when they present themselves.

Another important aspect of guiding cues is that they help us stay present. When we pay attention to our surroundings and are alert to the small changes happening around us, we stay more connected to the present moment. This connection allows us to respond more effectively to circumstances, as we are not reacting automatically or out of fear, but rather making decisions based on the information we are receiving at the moment.

On a day-to-day basis, this could be as simple as noticing how you feel when interacting with certain people. If an interaction leaves you feeling uncomfortable, that could be a sign that something is not right and that you should reconsider that relationship or the way you are communicating. Instead of ignoring those sensations, paying attention to them will help you better navigate your relationships and make decisions that are more aligned with your well-being.

Finally, it's worth remembering that guiding signs are tools, not certainties, and they help us maintain a healthy perspective. It's not about constantly looking for signs or interpreting every little event as a message from the universe. It's about being open and aware, being able to notice when something particularly catches our attention, and using that information to make more informed decisions.

The stream of variants is always in motion, and we can navigate it gracefully and effectively if we learn to listen to the signs it offers us. Over time, this practice of being attentive to signs becomes a natural way of interacting with the world, allowing us to flow with life rather than fight against it.

Let it go

Let's learn to stop exerting excessive control over every detail of life and instead trust that the natural flow of events can get us where we need to be. The mind, obsessed with common sense and the desire for control, often becomes the most difficult obstacle to well-being as it constantly attempts to adjust reality to match a predefined script. This "predefined script" refers to the rigid planning the mind makes about how events should unfold, with detailed expectations that attempt to maintain a tight grip on reality. Despite this, this struggle often leads to more problems and frustrations.

Zeland explains that the stream of variants already has the solutions we seek, if only we would allow ourselves to loosen our grip and let events unfold on their own. When the mind tries to keep everything under control, it generates excessive potentials and resistance, which attracts unnecessary problems. Instead, Zeland proposes that we let go, which means letting problems resolve themselves without direct intervention, whenever possible. In this way, unnecessary tension is removed, and the natural flow is allowed to find the most appropriate solution.

To illustrate this concept, let's consider an example from everyday life: Imagine you're organizing a surprise party, and you want everything to be perfect. You've planned every detail meticulously, from the decorations to the food to the exact time when the guest of honor will arrive. However, on the day of the event, unexpected events occur: one of the guests arrives late, the food takes longer than expected, and some of the decorations fall apart.

If you insist that everything go exactly as planned, you'll become stressed and not enjoy the moment. On the other hand, if you let go and allow the party to flow naturally, you'll be able to relax and enjoy the event with others, even if everything doesn't go as you imagined. The result could be even better than expected because you've allowed yourself and others to enjoy themselves without the pressure of absolute control.

In the context of trading, "going with the flow" means letting go of trying to control every market move. Many novice traders try to predict every fluctuation and become frustrated when the market doesn't follow their predictions. This need for control can lead to poor decisions, such as overtrading or failing to close a losing position in time. Instead, an experienced trader understands that they can't control the market; they can only control their reaction to it. By letting go of attachment and accepting that the market will do what it needs to do, a trader can make more rational, less impulsive decisions, adjusting to changing conditions without creating unnecessary stress.

Letting go of excessive control doesn't mean being passive or resigning yourself to any outcome. It's a balance between taking action when necessary and allowing the natural flow of events to continue without unnecessary intervention. It involves observing more and controlling less, shifting the center of gravity from absolute control to trusting the flow of life. By doing this, we gain a broader perspective, which allows us to identify opportunities and solve problems in a more effective and less draining way.

An important aspect of this approach is understanding how excessive importance moves us away from well-being. When we assign too much importance to a situation, we generate excessive potentials, which attract balancing forces that end up complicating things.

By reducing importance and letting go of the situation, we eliminate these potentials and allow the solution to come more easily and naturally. If you're in a job interview, and you're too worried about impressing the interviewer, that tension could work against you. But if you let go of the situation, you allow yourself to be yourself and flow with the conversation, which increases the chances of making a good impression.

In short, letting go is an art that requires trust in the flow of life and a willingness to loosen control when necessary. It frees us from the constant burden of trying to keep everything under control, allowing problems to resolve themselves naturally and life to surprise us with solutions we might not have imagined. It is an approach that invites us to go with the flow rather than fight against it, thus finding a more harmonious and effective path toward our goals.

We have reached the end of this book, a journey that has been both a trip of introspection and an opportunity to share with you everything I have learned during my journey as a trader. This journey has not been easy. It was full of obstacles, failures, learnings and, most importantly, moments of deep personal and professional growth. Trading, as I have tried to convey in these pages, is much more than strategies and technical analysis; it is a constant dance between the mind, emotions and the environment.

I would like to close this chapter with this personal reflection and a deep gratitude to all the people who, in one way or another, have been a fundamental part of my story. This book is also for you, who have been by my side, trusting in me when even I was doubtful. To Iván, Uziel, Adrián and Luis, my friends who always supported me in moments of uncertainty. To my family, for their patience and constant love. My wife Itzia, my tireless companion, who never left my side despite the difficulties, and encouraged me to keep going when everything seemed lost. And to Leonardo, whose support and faith in my abilities were key to getting to where I am today.

Thanks to each one of you, this dream of being a trader has become a reality. Thank you for believing in me, for trusting in my ability to manage your resources and, above all, for walking with me in this challenge of navigating the complex seas of the market. Every loss, every triumph and every learning are also yours.

| "We are the sum of the people we help shine"

If this book has brought you something valuable or has resonated with you, I invite you to leave a review on the platform where you purchased it. Your opinion will not only help me to continue improving, but it will allow this message to reach more people who, like you, may find something useful in these pages. It doesn't matter if it's brief; each comment is an opportunity for others to discover this content.

Thanks again, and may your journey continue to be filled successfully.

www.ingramcontent.com/pod-product-compliance
Lightning Source LLC
Chambersburg PA
CBHW031418210526
45464CB00005B/1942